THRIVING!

Not Just Surviving

Leading Your Law Firm to Excellence

SANDRA J. BOYER AND MICHAEL S. BEAVER
EDITORS

AMERICAN BAR ASSOCIATION
Tort Trial and Insurance
Practice Section

Cover design by Mary Anne Kulchawik/ABA Design

Printed in the United States of America.

29 28 27 26 25 5 4 3 2 1

Library of Congress Cataloging-in-Publication Data

Names: Boyer, Sandra J. editor | Beaver, Michael S. editor

Title: Thriving not surviving : leading your law firm to excellence / Sandra J. Boyer and Michael S. Beaver, Editors.

Description: Chicago : American Bar Association, 2025. | Summary: "Predictions of the dissolving small to midsize firm have been circulating so long that many have normalized the concept and consider it fact rather than a prophecy. "Small to midsize law firms will cease to exist in the next few years." "Large law firms will acquire small to midsize law firms until they no longer appear in the legal industry." "Only mega firms will be part of the future." Have these predictions come true, or is this some kind of self-fulfilling prophecy? To prevent such a decline, small to midsize law firms must make the conscious decision to address underlying factors that put them at risk. They must not buy-in to these age-old predictions but rather be managed more intentionally, more effectively, and with more awareness than their upsized industry competitors. Firm awareness is necessary. Firms must take stock of their strengths, their weaknesses, and stay vigilant when it comes to their progress--keeping an open mind when it comes to assessing challenges and opportunities. It's much like the fable of the tortoise and the hare. While big firms may be perceived as having more resources and therefore better opportunities to progress and persist, we know that small to midsize firms are more highly motivated, strive to be better prepared, stay focused, study their competition, do not shy away from effort, and continue to modify their performance to steadily increase their success. Managing a small to midsize law firm requires considerable ingenuity"-- Provided by publisher.

Identifiers: LCCN 2025021449 | ISBN 9781639056316 paperback | ISBN 9781639056323 epub

Subjects: LCSH: Law offices--United States | Law firms--United States | Law--Vocational guidance--United States

Classification: LCC KF318 .T47 2025 | DDC 340.068/4--dc23/eng/20250505

LC record available at https://lccn.loc.gov/2025021449

Discounts are available for books ordered in bulk. Special consideration is given to state bars, CLE programs, and other bar-related organizations. Inquire at Book Publishing, ABA Publishing, American Bar Association, 321 N. Clark Street, Chicago, Illinois 60654–7598.

www.shopABA.org

Contents

About the Editors ... *v*
About the Authors ... *vii*
Preface ... *xi*

Chapter 1: **Law Firm Culture** ... **1**

Chapter 2: **Client Relationships** ... **11**

Chapter 3: **Visibility Enhancement Programs** ... **19**

Chapter 4: **Attorney Recruiting and Retention** ... **31**

Chapter 5: **Meaningful Lawyer Development as a Tool for Success** ... **41**

Chapter 6: **Establishing and Managing Effective Practice Groups** ... **57**

Chapter 7: **Leadership in Law Firms** ... **65**

Chapter 8: **Risk Management and the Role of Law Firm General Counsel** ... **75**

Chapter 9: **Financial Management** ... **89**

Chapter 10: **Compensation Strategies for Law Firms** ... **103**

Chapter 11: The Role of Technology in the Modern Legal Landscape. 137

Chapter 12: Cybersecurity and Data Privacy for Law Firms 151

Chapter 13: Law Firm Succession Planning 165

Chapter 14: Generation to Generation 185

Chapter 15: Equipping Your Law Firm for the Future. 189

About the Editors

Sandra J. Boyer is the Founder and President of Legus International. For more than 30 years she has directed the efforts of this international organization to provide its members with cutting-edge legal industry educational programming and vision. Sandra has also spent more than 30 years providing legal management consulting strategies and vision to small to mid-size law firms around the world. Sandra has written numerous law practice management books and articles and has presented worldwide regarding the same topic. She was inducted into the College of Law Practice Management in 2003 for her contribution to the legal industry.

Michael S. Beaver was a partner for over 30 years in Holland & Hart LLP, a Denver-based firm with about 500 lawyers in offices throughout the Mountain West. He was involved in firm management roles most of that time. Mike is now semi-retired and serves as Senior Pro Bono Counsel to the firm. He is a Fellow of the American College of Employee Benefits Counsel, has served as an adjunct professor at the University of Denver Sturm College of Law, and is active in the leadership of the American Bar Association's Tort Trial & Insurance Practice Section. He is a graduate of the University of Colorado and the University of Denver Sturm College of Law.

About the Authors

Daniel J. Caruso was formerly a partner in the law firm of Simon, Peragine, Smith and Redfearn in New Orleans, from which he retired in 2023 and now serves as Of Counsel to the firm. He is a graduate of the Tulane School of law and has practiced actively for over 50 years in both criminal and civil arenas. His civil practice involved all types of liability issues ranging from general civil to maritime and has included advising clients on myriad insurance issues as well. He continues to be a member of the ABA, the Louisiana State Bar and several federal bars. He is also now embarking on career in mediation.

Breana Jackson is a graduate of the Central Michigan University (CMU) Leadership Institute as well as the LeaderShape Institute. She has attended leadership conferences and workshops for the past 15 years and has trained thousands of undergraduates in leadership facilitation and implementation. Since 2019, Jackson has been focusing on leadership development within the legal industry. Currently, Jackson serves as the Vice President of Legus International, a global network of small to mid-size law firms focused on client service, education, and camaraderie.

Brian Kennel, CEO and Founder of PerformLaw, has spent over 20 years helping law firms run smarter, more competitive practices. He understands firsthand the challenges of managing a firm—balancing growth, profitability, and efficiency—because he's been in the thick of it himself. As a former legal administrator and entrepreneur who built and sold a law firm management services company to a Fortune 500 company, Brian brings real-world experience to every engagement. He takes a hands-on, practical approach to helping firms make data-driven decisions, optimize performance, and plan for long-term success. His goal is simple: to take the guesswork out of running a law firm so his clients can focus on what they do best—practicing law.

Colin S. Levy is General Counsel at Malbek, where he was the company's first legal hire and helped scale its contract lifecycle management platform from startup to global enterprise. A graduate of Boston College Law School, Colin began his legal journey during the 2008 recession, opting for in-house work over big law. He leveraged his early paralegal experience in e-discovery to build a career at the intersection of law and technology.

A leading voice in legal innovation, he has contributed to numerous books and publications, including authoring *The Legal Tech Ecosystem*, co-authoring *CLM for Dummies*, and editing *The Legal Tech Handbook*. Colin is also an Adjunct Professor of Law at Albany Law School, serves as a judge for the American Legal Technology Awards, and is a monthly columnist *for Today's General Counsel.*

Known for his practical, unvarnished voice on legal tech and AI, Colin is committed to making technology usable and useful for legal professionals. He regularly advises companies on AI and champions tools that solve real problems rather than chase hype. Based in the Berkshires, he writes, speaks, and invests in the future of legal tech.

Eric B. Levine is a shareholder and the President of Lindabury McCormick Estabrook & Cooper, where he concentrates his practice on commercial litigation, cyber-security/data privacy, and probate litigation. He represents business owners and individuals in a wide range of business, real estate, and personal litigation while also providing counsel and acting as a trusted advisor. He is a presenting Faculty Member at Rutgers University and has written and presented seminars on data privacy issues, commercial real estate, and construction, among other topics. He has been named a Best's Lawyer, and an ROI Influencer multiple times.

Matthew Moeller has handled maritime matters throughout the Gulf South, the Pacific Northwest, the Midwest, and the Eastern Seaboard. Matthew regularly defends Jones Act, Longshore Harbor, and Worker's Compensation Act, and general maritime personal injury claims, and both defends and prosecutes maritime contractual disputes and maritime property damage matters. He also represents underwriters and marine insurers in insurance coverage matters. Matthew's experience also includes the defense of insurers, hotel operators, and transportation companies in land-based personal injury actions. He is the owner and managing attorney of The Moeller Firm in New Orleans, Louisiana.

Ronald L. Richman is a shareholder at Bullivant Houser Bailey PC ("Bullivant Houser") in its San Francisco, California. Ron also serves as the inhouse General Counsel to Bullivant Houser, and has previously served on its Board of Directors. Ron started his legal career in the US Navy JAGC, stationed at the former Naval Station, Treasure Island, San Francisco. Ron is a member of his firm's Business Litigation Practice Group. His practice includes representing ERISA Multi-Employer Taft-Hartley Trust Funds and advising homeowners and title insurance companies in a wide range of real estate, title, and property boundary disputes, across the state of California. Over Ron's 30+ year involvement in TIPS, he served on the TIPS Council and is a former Chair of the Insurance Coverage Litigation Committee, Vice-Chair of the Business Litigation Committee, and former Vice-Chair of the Fidelity & Surety Law Committee.

Chuck Roberts helps law firms increase their revenue and profitability by elevating the capabilities of their partners and attorneys with training and coaching, and by providing operational consulting for implementing best practices. He is a transformational leader who has served as CEO, COO, and Corporate Director of Business Development (leading Marketing and Sales) for national and international professional services firms, and serves as a Fractional C-Level leader for firms in transition. He's also an internationally recognized expert on the science of persuasive communication and a professional ghostwriter of competitive proposals and presentations. Chuck is the Founder, President, and CEO of Performance Management Group, Inc.

Richard J. Wittbrodt is a senior equity partner at Gibbs Giden Locher Turner Senet & Wittbrodt LLC in Los Angeles, California, and has been with the firm since 1987. His primary focus has been in construction litigation, including prosecuting and defending claims of delay, disruption, defective construction, mechanic's lien and stop payment notice foreclosure actions, for both public and private projects for both owners and contractors. Mr. Wittbrodt was the managing partner of the firm for 16 years responsible for the reporting and evaluation of the firm's financial performance. He is currently a member of his firm's executive committee. He is a fellow of the American College of Construction Lawyers and is Chair of the ABA's Forum on Construction Law's finance committee. Prior to law school Mr. Wittbrodt was a practicing C.P.A. and was a CFO of a real estate development firm in Los Angeles and went on to receive his *Juris Doctor* from Pepperdine University Caruso School of Law. He has an M.B.A. (Tax) from Golden Gate University and obtained his B.B.A. from the University of Michigan.

Preface

Predictions of the dissolving small to mid-size firm have been circulating so long that many have normalized the concept and consider it fact rather than a prophecy.

- "Small to midsize law firms will cease to exist in the next few years."
- "Large law firms will acquire small to midsize law firms until they no longer appear in the legal industry."
- "Only mega firms will be part of the future."

Have these predictions come true, or is this some kind of self-fulfilling prophecy? To prevent such a decline, small to mid-size law firms must make the conscious decision to address underlying factors that put them at risk. They must not buy-in to these age-old predictions but rather be managed more intentionally, more effectively, and with more awareness than their upsized industry competitors. Firm awareness is necessary. Firms must take stock of their strengths, their weaknesses, and stay vigilant when it comes to their progress—keeping an open mind when it comes to assessing challenges and opportunities. It's much like the fable of the tortoise and the hare. While big firms may be perceived as having more resources and therefore better opportunities to progress and persist, we know that small to mid-size firms are more highly motivated, strive to be better prepared, stay focused, study their competition, do not shy away from effort, and continue to modify their performance to steadily increase their success. Managing a small to mid-size law firm requires considerable ingenuity.

Focused on practical, cutting-edge, and experience-driven knowledge, the following chapters will map how small to mid-size law firms may effectively address current and rising management techniques to create a strong foundation capable of proactively serving clients and running a law firm as a productive business. For more than 30 years, I have consulted with law firm partners, associates, administration, and management leaders to create, implement, and modify business operations to ensure they can successfully meet the changing needs of clients and demands of business.

My purpose in creating this reference is to share the knowledge and experience of experts in the field who have extensive practical experience and want to share that with others. The authors are—or have been—managing partners, executive committee members, practicing lawyers, law firm management consultants, and other professionals who have displayed steady success throughout their decades of engagement with the small to mid-size legal community. While the information is primarily geared toward small to mid-size law firms, it actually provides insightful business strategies that can be implemented easily, updated as needed, and modified culturally for success in any law firm and within any practice.

Each chapter may be utilized to inform and direct firms on the titled topic. Additionally, each chapter's information may be used together to develop a comprehensive guide for overall effective law firm management.

While it is important to understand the positive attributes, practical strategies, useful techniques, and effective steps that can be implemented for success, perhaps it is as important to understand what can undermine law firm success. Negative factors causing many law firms to fail are greed, lack of collegiality, self-importance, lack of vision, an internal-only focus, and lack of client-centered interest. Firms that maintain a consistent focus on business operations in addition to practicing law and serving clients often remain more successful and profitable than those firms who do not.

The guidance and information in this book can help your firm create a business-focused culture profitable for everybody, including staff, administration, lawyers, owners, and non-owners. It will promote buying into the idea of planned success and the role each person plays in quality client service, effective business operation, and long-term individual and firm success. Pursuing a career in the legal industry is not for the faint of heart. Intentionally integrating planning and focus is a smarter, not harder way to maintain stamina and resilience on the path to success.

Strategic planning is not included as a titled chapter in this book. Strategic planning is made up of all the areas vital to managing a law firm. As you read through the chapters of this book, consider the following:

1. The Firm's Vision—A law firm's vision statement shares what you want your firm to accomplish in the future for an identified period of time. It identifies what success looks like for the firm.
2. The Firm's Mission—The mission identifies the firm's purpose, what sets it apart, and how it strives to operate. The mission should set the foundation that guides your firm's decision making and strategy.
3. Utilization of the Firm's Strengths
4. Awareness of the Firm's Weaknesses
5. Identification of the Firm's Opportunities
6. Identification of Threats to the Firm's Success
7. Establishment of the Firm's Goals (for the next 3–5 years)
8. Steps Needed to Reach the Firm's Goals

Use the information shared in these chapters to help you develop your strategic plan. Consistently implement the strategic plan. Update the strategic plan regularly and as needed.

Our authors will challenge and encourage you to be client-focused, utilize innovative thinking, build internal and external relationships, be proactive, consider potential outcomes and make plans to meet your goals, construct a team, plan consistently, use your talents, and celebrate success. Remember, the tortoise has the potential to live up to 100 times longer than the hare, but he doesn't do it by just sitting still.

Sandra Boyer

Chapter 1
Law Firm Culture

Defining the Firm's Destiny

Michael S. Beaver

> *We are what we repeatedly do.*
>
> —Aristotle (maybe)

I have just retired after 38 years at a single medium-size regional law firm. Yes, I know, that kind of longevity makes me a dinosaur. But I really haven't spent my professional life in one place because I'm old-school; frictionless lateral mobility has been a feature of the legal talent market for many years now. I can easily sum up what attracted me to my firm, and what has kept me there for nearly 40 years: my firm's culture.

I was attracted to the firm from the beginning because I immediately identified with the consistent values and traits evidenced by those who interviewed me. I had an immediate strong sense of what the firm was like, and that, to put it simply, these were my peeps. In the years since, I've felt an equally strong sense of identification with and pride in the firm.

On top of the personal satisfaction, I've gotten from belonging to my firm, its culture has provided a compelling business benefit—a true competitive advantage. One of my late career experiences provides one example, but nowhere near the only one. A few years ago I was asked by a very large, industry-leading company to assemble a team of lawyers to make a pitch to take over the defense of a lawsuit with eight-figure exposure. The company was considering a number of other firms, from national to local in size. For our pitch I brought in five colleagues. We made a presentation which turned into a lively discussion with the prospective client representatives about strategy, staffing, and desired outcomes.

We got the work. The senior client representative at our pitch told me it was because she had never seen a team of lawyers exhibit such mutual respect and synergy. This wasn't a one-time performance by our team. It was the result of years of similar experiences with one another which reinforced our firm's values and identity. Culture paid.

My purpose isn't to brag on my firm—although even now I'm happy to do that. Rather, I think my experience illustrates the many ways that firm culture can deliver success to a law firm, and real meaning and satisfaction to its lawyers. In this chapter I will attempt to break down that proposition into its components, and provide some ideas on building any law firm's culture.

What Do We Mean by the "Culture" of a Law Firm?

What is law firm culture, beyond the general idea of "I do/don't like it here," or "this is just the way things are done around here?" The APA's Dictionary of Psychology defines "organizational culture" as

> *a distinctive pattern of thought and behavior shared by the members of the same organization and reflected in their language, values, attitudes, beliefs and customs. The culture of an organization is in many ways analogous to the personality of an individual.*

No definition is perfect, but this one captures the essence. Culture is not a mission statement, or a set of aspirational principles, or a strategy, or set of goals. Culture expresses itself by both thought *and* behavior, as expressed in numerous, observable ways. While culture develops over time, it is expressed and experienced daily at all levels of an organization, in ways large and small.

There are several important **hard truths** about law firm culture:

- **Hard truth number one**: the culture of a law firm exists and develops whether or not management intends it. A law firm, like any other organization, has a culture whether it wants to or not. And that culture is expressed by inaction as much as action. Culture is an outcome, not an aspiration. Ignoring it won't make it go away.
- **Hard truth number two**: Culture is necessarily dynamic. It is always changing, influenced by sometimes uncontrollable

internal and external factors. For instance, consider the impact of COVID-19 on cultural factors (external) and various firms' reactions (internal) during that era. Profound changes in the legal services marketplace, and the evolving aspirations of young lawyers, provide other examples. Culture is a moving target.

- **Hard truth number three**: The impact of law firm culture doesn't end with lawyers and staff—it plays out in a firm's external image and reputation, its dealings with (and attractiveness to) clients, vendors, courts, competitors, and the rest of the world. As Gallup, the prominent polling and consulting group, has put it, "[c]ulture is the unique way that your organization lives out its company purpose and delivers on its brand promise to customers. . . . For this reason, a strong corporate culture functions as a differentiator in the marketplace."
- **Hard truth number four**: Law firm culture is profoundly influenced by factors outside the firm itself. Among professional practice firms (think lawyers, physicians, accountants, large consultancies, etc.), organizational culture is shaped in part by the overall culture of the profession *itself*, which is in turn shaped by courts, professional rules, regulators, and client expectations. And reinforced by these influences, lawyers (like physicians) have a longstanding separate professional culture centered on their own independence of judgment, and in many cases a confidence in the superiority of their skills over organizational priorities. This makes the development of a coherent law firm culture more challenging (cat-herding, anyone?).
- **Hard truth number five**: Culture can become ingrown. Those leaders and other principals who shape culture can become focused only on internal factors, oblivious to the fact that culture inevitably affects client and other "outside" relations. A related danger is commonly known as groupthink—the acceptance of behaviors and norms without the freedom to question or challenge the approach the firm takes to various difficult issues, eventually leading to the weakened ability to even identify different approaches.

What Difference Does Law Firm Culture Make?

If individual happiness and satisfaction isn't enough, what else can a positive law firm culture provide? There are well-documented answers.

The Gallup organization, via survey, found that only 22% of employees in all organizations (not just law firms) felt connected to the employer's culture. There isn't any reason to believe that law firms are an exception.

As to this slightly-less-than-one-quarter contingent, what benefits does an organization realize? Gallup's studies support the notion that those who feel connected to culture are much more likely to be meaningfully engaged in their work and to recommend the workplace to others. They are much *less* likely to report frequent burnout, or to look for outside employment opportunities.

In sum, the stronger an organization's culture, the more likely it is to be successful by a number of objective measures, such as profitability and long-term success. That may beg the question as to what makes for a "strong" culture, but the point could be too easily lost.

A recent survey conducted by a major legal recruitment firm found that culture trumps even compensation when partners decide whether to stay in a firm or leave, and if they leave, where they go. In an age of regular partner mobility, this is perhaps the most vital evidence we have of culture's actual business impact.

Finally, understanding law firm culture is vital for almost all management purposes. With a realistic grasp of firm culture, leaders are equipped to affect the direction of the firm. They can develop strategies for nurturing the positive aspects of the firm's culture (they exist; otherwise the firm wouldn't), and affecting whatever changes in culture are desired (most often measured by the delta between what the firm aspires to be, and what it is).

How Do We Evaluate Law Firm Culture?

Lawyers are quite familiar with the "you'll know it when you see it" formulation. We all dealt with it in a memorable Constitutional Law class session. For better or worse, it is a phrase many apply—not without reason—to law firm culture. It is indeed difficult to articulate what makes up the concept of any organization's culture.

But for those charged with the management of a law firm, "you'll know it when you see it" isn't a very helpful standard. We have to do our best to articulate the ways in which a given firm's culture is defined and experienced. So, at the risk of leaving out something significant, here are the major culture drivers:

- **Commonly expressed statements of purpose vs. implicitly understood "purpose."** Most successful firms have taken the time to articulate their key values. But even in the absence of express values, lawyers and staff will imply the firm's purposes. Those implied understandings will likely be cynical, and very well may be accurate.
- **Behavior of law firm leaders (both designated and informal leaders).** Values, goals and purposes are meaningless if law firm leaders (and those in the firm who lead without title) don't live them by example and reinforcement. Actually, it's worse than that. If the actions and inactions of leaders are inconsistent with stated values, the result is widespread cynicism.
- **Tolerance or intolerance of digression from expressed values and purposes.** Inevitably there will be individual behavior inconsistent with the firm's stated purposes and values. What are the consequences? The answer is a powerful determinant of firm culture. Example: "We don't tolerate explosive anger or bullying." What are the consequences of violating that stated norm? Are there consequences affecting compensation or recognition?
- **Frequency, transparency, and clarity of communications.** People naturally yearn for information about things that affect their lives. In the absence of facts, human nature supplies explanations and narratives—often on the cynical side. Does firm leadership get ahead of events (and other stressors) by communicating, as honestly as possible and as soon as possible, what things mean for the firm and its constituents? Are communications clear, or clouded by "corporate speak" (another term that I suppose we know when we see it).
- **Shared sense of purpose (ultimately pride and identification).** Are lawyers and staff able to articulate what makes the firm different? Do they identify personally with the differentiators? Ultimately, are they proud to be a part of the organization?
- **Long-term vs. short-term orientation.** This is a distinction well-known in large American corporate circles. No matter what it says it is doing, does the organization focus primarily on short-term objectives, or does it meaningfully incorporate long-term goals? Do the organization's plans reflect an actual focus on the long-term vs. the current, or next year's, performance?

- **Stories and myths.** Many firms have stories—hopefully truthful, sometimes semi-apocryphal—about events which have formed the organization's purpose and identity. Often these are stories about the law firm's founders. In my experience, I've heard a number of these stories about my firm and its founders, and found important value in them.
- **Awards and recognition.** Does the firm actively seek out and recognize examples of behaviors that exemplify its values, principles, and aspirations? This can be a powerful way to identify and reinforce desired behaviors. Example—My firm has an award, given every year or so, to an individual lawyer who most exemplifies the values and behaviors of one of our founders (which have clearly laid a foundation for our firm's culture). People notice.
- **Personal vs. organizational buy-in.** As mentioned above, professionals—especially lawyers and physicians—have a sense of purpose, ability, and mission that transcends the organization to which they belong. It's inevitable. But the most effective law firm cultures are able to tap into that individual sense of mission, so that lawyers see that the firm is so aligned with their own values that there could be no better platform for their practices.
- **Inward vs. external vs. balanced focus.** Some organizations become so sure of themselves that they begin to focus almost entirely on their own strengths, ignoring or minimizing what their clients and other outsiders experience. On the other hand, an organization can become so focused on the perceived needs of clients and outsiders that the interests of its own members are minimized. Neither approach will deliver long-term success. A law firm's culture ideally reflects a balance between the interests of its lawyers and staff, and clients and other outside entities.
- **Distribution of power within the organization: centralized/decentralized.** In short, how distant do lawyers and staff feel from the levers of power? Is authority granted mainly to one person, or several? Are there leaders at ground level whom lawyers and staff believe have (1) an interest in their concerns, and (2) the ability to influence ultimate decisions?
- **Individual and organization generosity.** How willing are lawyers and staff to help others within the firm, without expectation of reward, by mentoring, sharing knowledge and experience, making introductions, etc.? Generosity is a key driver of culture, and profoundly affects law firm integration and turnover.

- **Teamwork vs. individual silos.** Does the firm actively expect and encourage teamwork in both the delivery of client service and the marketing of the firm? Or is success measured principally on an individual basis?
- **Degree of support of lawyers and staff in situations of personal difficulty.** Here's a real rubber-meets-the-road factor. Personal difficulties—individual or family medical issues, divorce, family conflict, etc.—will be experienced by 100% of an organization's membership at some point. How does the firm respond when asked for time off, or some other accommodation, in difficult circumstances? Yes, there are demands occasionally posed which are beyond the bounds of reason, but most aren't. What does the firm do when confronted with them?

Assessing Your Law Firm's Culture

Firm leadership should begin by articulating, in as brief a fashion as possible, what it desires the firm culture to be.

With desired cultural traits identified, firm leadership must then assess its culture for what it is, not what its leaders wish it to be. Like any inquiry that calls on us to be objective, this is a difficult inquiry, but it is doable.

Many firms call upon a consultant to assist in cultural assessment, because the work necessarily requires objectivity. The process usually begins with leaders articulating what they believe the firm's culture to be. The leaders' perceived culture can then be measured against the perceptions of firm lawyers and staff. This is most often done by surveys (there are online templates, but to be effective they must be adapted), individual interviews, focus groups, and other forms of internal research.

What do firm leaders need to know? Whether the firm lives up to its stated purposes and aspirations? Can lawyers and staff articulate the firm's mission? Do leaders reflect it? If not, why not? Do the firm's management mechanics (performance management, compensation, etc.) reflect its stated values? What are the incentives or disincentives to act in accordance with the firm's values? Do lawyers and employees believe the firm actually delivers the client service and value to which it claims to aspire? Do lawyers and staff believe they receive meaningful, timely communications about the firm's aspirations and performance? Do they believe they are supported in their professional development, and their personal lives? Do they believe that they are part of meaningful teams focused on delivering client value? Do they believe that they receive adequate training and support?

Partners' views of cultural issues are very important. However, partners can become wrapped up in cultural aspirations (yes, I remember the rosy opening paragraphs of this chapter), and are not necessarily the most reliable cultural narrators. In general, leadership should assume that the higher the pay grade, the rosier the view will be. Some of the most stark, realistic views about firm culture will come from associates and staff.

The results will be, to some degree, contradictory. Leaders must face the results with objectivity, another process which can be aided by an outside consultant.

Cultural Change

As you would expect, this is the most difficult task of all. If leadership, after solid input from various stakeholders (which can include lawyers, staff, and for the most daring, even clients), concludes that some cultural change is desirable, how is it done? Some thoughts:

- Any attempt to change a firm's culture should begin by prominently highlighting the aspects of its culture which align with desired outcomes. Attempts to effect change will bring about anxiety and even resentment. Focusing on what the firm is already getting right helps alleviate these emotions, and promotes buy-in for needed changes.
- Recognize that cultural change is never immediate. It is a gradual, even incremental, process. The bigger the organization or firm, the longer actual change will take.
- Most law firm cultures have subcultures—usually defined by practice group, geographic location, level of seniority, and other factors. These subcultures should be identified, and serious consideration given to them, in any plan to effect cultural change.
- Create a new realistic, realizable cultural statement. Ideally it will overlap with past cultural or mission statements as much as possible. The firm must define, and clearly articulate, what its ultimate values are, and what principles will guide it into the future.
- Leaders must live according to the firm's statement of values and principles. Yes, this is incredibly obvious. But for some individuals and firms it is also very difficult. Leaders must exhibit what they expound. Otherwise, credibility is immediately diluted, and soon lost altogether.

- Make any changes necessary to align the firm's reward systems with its values and principles. This is also obvious and difficult. Will teamwork be valued as much as individually trumpeted results when it comes to client development? Will clearly inappropriate behaviors (bullying, anger, blame-casting, etc.) be tolerated and even rewarded?
- Recruitment should be consistent with, and even built upon, firm values and principles. If those things are consistently reflected in the beliefs and behaviors and firm members, it will positively affect all hiring decisions—from first-year associates to seasoned lateral partner candidates. A caveat here is that this should never lead to the "reproduction" of non-diverse lawyers within the organization. Recruitment and hiring must be driven by the principle that shared values and beliefs can and will be built across genders, ethnicities, and other characteristics—not just among those who "look like us."

Summary

Your law firm's culture is a vital determinant—maybe the most important one—of the firm's long-term success. Understanding and affecting culture will not only guide the firm in its delivery of client services, it will significantly impact lawyer recruitment, retention, satisfaction, and overall firm health.

Chapter 2
Client Relationships

Matthew Moeller

Identifying and Finding Potential Clients

Before establishing a client relationship, you need to ask yourself a simple question: who do I want to represent? Generally, you will seek clients that fit within a specific area of your or your firm's practice or within a range of areas in which you have expertise. For example, if you are an energy litigator, you might seek out both upstream and downstream companies in the energy sector, their insurers, contractors, and other companies that service the industry. However, if you are a lawyer primarily representing individuals in divorce cases or trust and estate matters, you may focus more on individuals and families, and you may not be as actively engaged in seeking clients through direct personal contact since nobody wants to encourage divorce and press people into end-of-life decisions. A prominent presence in the community and membership and leadership roles in family law groups and organizations may be a good way to identify potential clients or for you to be identified as a lawyer that community members may want to work with. For a plaintiff's lawyer, the most effective way to solicit clients might be radio, television, and internet marketing within a certain county, city, region, or nationwide.

Once you identify the types of clients you desire to represent and work with, the question becomes where do you find those potential clients, and how do you ultimately turn those potential clients into your existing clients? Local, state, and national bar associations that include other lawyers in similar practice areas, in-house attorneys, and corporate and in-house risk managers are good places to identify potential clients and people that can connect you with potential clients. I have often heard other lawyers scoff at investing time in bar associations, seeing other attorney members as nothing more than "competitors," but such a view is short-sighted. Those "competitors" can also be clients when local counsel is needed, referral sources in conflicts, and great references if a potential client calls them to vet you.

Targeted industry organizations can also be fruitful places to identify potential clients. There are countless advocacy organizations, associations, and other similar groups devoted to a vast range of industries that promote their industries and members, who generally are many of the most prominent businesses in that industry. Joining and becoming involved in one that supports an industry made up of organizations you desire to represent can be beneficial in providing opportunities to meet potential clients and industry colleagues of potential clients. Broader groups such as Rotary Clubs and Chambers of Commerce are full of businesses and individuals who can use legal services. Even more so than in a bar association, there is often a substantial investment of time and money required to position yourself to establish a potential client relationship with a member of such an organization. But, like anything else, the more you put in, the better your chance of getting something worthwhile.

Your community and social network are also valuable resources for identifying potential clients. Your neighbors could be business owners, accountants, attorneys in other practice areas, or even victims of a horrific accident. Your friends, other parents who have children in your kids' schools, others in a biking or running group, and those you went to high school, college, or law school with are all people who could be potential clients or assist you in identifying potential clients. When presented with an opportunity, do not be shy about enthusiastically explaining to people exactly what you do to help your clients and how you may be able to assist them or someone they might know.

Establishing the Relationship

Client development can be a long road. It takes the three p's: patience, persistence, and perseverance. The road often starts with a certain type of initial personal contact with a potential client, whether it be an email, phone call, face-to-face, or Zoom meeting, and the old adage that people desire to work with those they know, like, and trust rings especially true in the practice of law. Likewise, an introduction to a potential client through someone the potential client knows, likes, and trusts can be a very effective way to generate a productive initial contact. That could be a relative of the potential client, a close personal friend, or even a lawyer representing that potential client in another area of law. It could also be a trusted business advisor like the potential client's accountant, insurance agent, broker, or another professional service provider. A good faith ask to that person for an introduction demonstrates a sincere interest and desire to work with that potential client, and can be very effective in motivating the person to make an introduction eventually.

Professionally styled, personally tailored email correspondence can also be effective, but generally, in many practices, particularly on the corporate defense side, there really is no substitute for face-to-face contact, especially when it comes to an introduction. I once had a professional, non-lawyer mentor many years ago when I first entered the workforce and had some business development responsibility tell me "that it is always better to know someone," which has been true throughout my career. The best introductions and the most effective correspondence in making initial contacts with potential clients or those facilitated by someone the potential client knows, likes, and trusts.

As in life, timing can be everything in client development, so do not get discouraged if the early investment of time and effort seems futile. If you stay persistent, more likely than not, an opportunity will arise from any number of circumstances. It could be that the person who makes the decisions regarding legal representation and who may have had a long-standing existing relationship with another lawyer or law firm has moved on, and there is someone new in that role who does not have an established relationship with any lawyer. It could also be that, for whatever reason, an individual or organization is looking to change legal representation or maybe considering spreading the work around a little more.

A keen understanding of the client's business is critical; in most cases, defense litigation services end up in a line item or part of another line item on the organization's income statement at the end of the year. Your client or certain people in your client's organization are responsible for that line item, and you want to do your best to ensure that that line item reflects the value in whatever portion you contributed to that figure. In other words, what did the client get in return for your portion of that line item? Was it a favorable settlement, good outcomes on dispositive motions, a favorable verdict at trial, or were there cases that lingered far too long, lost opportunities to resolve matters favorably, or an unpredicted, adverse result at trial that you never saw coming or never informed the client of the potential risk?

When speaking with a prospective client, when the opportunity comes, and at the appropriate time, it is important that you can effectively communicate what makes you a good fit for this potential client and what you do that might be a little different from others that could bring this potential client a greater level of service, value, and a better client experience. Have you been particularly successful with early resolution of the potential client's matters or dispositive motions? Can you provide general reliability and predictability regarding the fees and expenses associated with the representation? If a case has to be tried, do you have sufficient experience and a baseline history that can provide the prospective client confidence in you and your firm's ability to take a case through trial and appeal if necessary? Being able to communicate exactly what you can offer effectively is critically important. Conversely, it is not a good idea to brag about personal or professional honors or an individual or a firm's self-perceived intellect or "win-loss" record as opposed to other firms, and it is certainly not worthwhile to badmouth other lawyers and law firms.

The successful establishment of an attorney-client relationship can often be fostered and developed partially through personal connections and shared interests. Try to find a way to connect with the prospective client on a personal level. Not everybody wants to talk about business all of the time. Maybe you work out at the same gym, have kids in school together, go to the same church, went to the same college, or both of you may be into hunting, fishing, or sailing. Personal commonality can be a great building block in the early stages of a potential attorney-client relationship. Most potential clients will either ask you for something in writing detailing your and your firm's experience, rates, and other information after an initial meeting or at some point in the future. It is always a good idea to have a general letter on file with this information that can be revised quickly to fit different clients and situations and sent to the potential client. Providing two to three client references that the prospective client would be familiar with is also beneficial.

First impressions are so important. Upon receipt of the first case, specific assignment, or other type of project, be responsive, grateful, and excited about the new opportunity to work with this client. You should set clear expectations; what are the client's ultimate objectives? Is this a litigation matter that needs to be quickly resolved or possibly tried? Are there budgetary objectives or concerns, and to the extent not already understood, if you need the help of other professionals in your office, you should get authority for them to work on the matter. What deliverables will you provide? Will it be a draft of a contract or a high-level legal memorandum to serve as guidance on an issue? Or perhaps a demand letter, or a general defense or prosecution of a claim? You should always have a plan and be ready to make a recommendation to fit any scenario.

Managing the Relationship

Like any other relationship, in an attorney-client relationship, communication is key. You should communicate early and often! Be as active and as frequent in communication as possible. One of the things I most commonly hear from young lawyers when I encourage them to communicate more frequently with clients or even opposing counsel is: "I do not want to bother them." In nearly 20 years of practice, I have never had a client or opposing counsel request that I communicate less frequently. Personally, I like to receive follow-up emails from anyone, whether it be a professional services provider, opposing counsel, or even my wife, following up on something I need to do on the home front! However, I do not like to see emails from clients inquiring about the status of a matter because those emails should not have to be sent.

Understand that clients, like the rest of us, are busy people. Email is a great, efficient, and effective way to communicate, but emails to clients should be succinct, issue-focused, and easy to read. Also, do not forget that the telephone is your friend; a lawyer should not be afraid to pick up the telephone and call a client if they find it challenging to reach the client through email. It is usually never personal and results from the client being busy and already having to manage a heavy email load. Sometimes, it just may be easier to catch them on the off chance by telephone. The great thing about the telephone is that it is a more informal setting, and depending on time, there may be an opportunity for the conversation to veer off on to other issues or subjects where there may be an opportunity to talk briefly about something of interest to you, the client, or you both that can be a building block in a more personal relationship. When communicating with a client, you always want to try to be positive, upbeat, and optimistic, as most people do not like to communicate with those who appear to always be in a bad mood or irritated by something. However, you have to be candid, and your obligation to be candid can sometimes temper your desire and need to be positive.

My father, also an attorney, who is still practicing today, told me years ago, when I was a teenager, that his clients do not like surprises; therefore, he does not like surprises! Not surprisingly, throughout my legal career, I have learned, too, that my clients do not like surprises. So, to say that I inherited my dad's view of surprises, for better or worse, would be an understatement. Active, frequent, and candid communication can help limit client surprises. In my experience, the things that would often get attorneys into trouble in terms of surprising their clients generally either had to do with underestimated fees and expenses or a case evaluation that did not adequately prepare a client for a significant adverse result. Often, those two can go hand-in-hand.

Keeping your eye out for recent developments that impact your client is a great way to maintain continuous engagement, regardless of whether or not you have an active matter with that client alerting the clients of new legislation, a new article on an issue of interest, or a suit filed against a competitor or a similar organization involving a claim or legal theory that the client should be concerned about or all great ways to keep the lines of communication open. When notifying the client of such a development, think about trying to succinctly explain how it potentially affects the client, and in many situations, it may be worthwhile to volunteer to give a presentation, write a comprehensive memo, or have an informal conference call on the issue.

Seeking out opportunities for personal contact is another way to stay engaged. That could mean maybe going out of the way to meet a client in the area when you may be traveling for other reasons, including a vacation. Most clients enjoy face-to-face contact with their attorneys and are open to meeting for lunch, a cup of coffee, or visiting their office if you are in the area.

Going the extra mile when an opportunity to help presents itself is also a great way to show your personal investment in the relationship. When I was in undergraduate school, my marketing professor relayed a story about a former student of his who was a young insurance salesman. The former student had been pursuing a large client for some time, and the client confided in the former student that the business of his and his wife's jobs was starting to take a toll on their marriage. The former student, realizing he had kids the same age as the prospective client, offered to take the prospective client's kids for the weekend and encouraged the prospective client to take his wife on a weekend getaway somewhere. The prospective client took him up on the offer and, not surprisingly, became an actual client soon thereafter. The fact that the former student took the kids for the weekend may not necessarily have been 100% of the reason that he ultimately converted the prospective client into an actual client, but there is no doubt that it helped his chances compared to others because it demonstrated a real interest in the prospective client as a person.

You also want to show that you are interested in clients as people and their professional growth. Seek out opportunities to invite clients to speak on panels you may be moderating, conferences you may be helping to plan, or to provide introductions or opportunities for them to meet other like-minded folks in their industry. Bad results and big mistakes happen, and you have to take responsibility. Clients understand that lawyers are human and that nobody is perfect, but they also do not have a lot of patience for lawyers that are unaccountable, and blame others, particularly their own colleagues, and are afraid to take the blame and give their clients bad news. Admitting mistakes, showing imperfection, but then proposing a best-case scenario solution and achieving that solution under bad circumstances can sometimes work to strengthen a relationship even more than a good result.

Chapter 3
Visibility Enhancement Programs

Chuck Roberts

Overview

It's no secret that one way to become a hero at a law firm is by bringing in lots of work. But not all work is equivalent. To improve your firm's stability, it's important to expand and diversify your client base. And, to improve your firm's financial performance, it's important to pursue work that will enable you to simultaneously increase revenue and profitability, overcome client sensitivity to fees, and provide a good return on your investment in business development because there is a substantial cost associated with winning work.

Thus, the investment of your firm's human and financial resources in business development activities should be directed at those approaches likely to produce favorable results. Marketing and sales strategies, tactics, and techniques characterized by a high likelihood of producing desired outcomes are based on science. Do they work as intended 100% of the time? No. They are science, not magic, but focusing on approaches that have been demonstrated to produce better results a higher percentage of the time can help you achieve a higher return on your investment in business development activities and enhance morale, because it's always more fun to win than lose an opportunity. Winning more frequently also tends to encourage your attorneys to do more business development.

Aiming for the Right Target

The most effective approach for simultaneously growing your firm's revenue and profitability depends on the type of law you practice and the characteristics of your ideal client. For example, the approach most likely to produce results when pursuing corporate clients engaged in large land development projects will be different than the approach most likely to produce desired results when practicing personal injury law, where your ideal client might be characterized as a middle-aged, middle-income individual. With this in mind, following is a discussion of effective business development techniques as applied to the two major client sectors: organizations and individuals. It's recommended that you characterize your ideal clients in detail and then use that information to fine-tune your approach within the sector that applies to your firm. Unfortunately, there are too many variations and combinations of characteristics to address all of them in this resource.

Expanding Your Client Base within the Organizational Market Sector

There are three principal methods for expanding your client base within the organizational market sector, and they vary substantially in their effectiveness, lag time between prospect contact and obtaining a contract, and cost of implementation. These three methods are as follows.

Pull Marketing

Pull marketing gets its name from the fact that it draws clients to your firm. It is by far the most effective, fastest, and least-cost method for expanding and diversifying your client base, yet it's generally the most misapplied, underutilized, and poorly coordinated approach. Its two forms are delivering presentations and writing articles, with delivering presentations being orders of magnitude more effective than writing articles. Many law firms encourage their attorneys to develop and deliver presentations at conferences, and in some cases provide a financial incentive, but few firms recognize the power of pull marketing so most lack a deliberate, well-crafted pull marketing program, and the individuals who do develop and deliver such presentations at those firms make considerable errors in their approach.

First, to fully leverage the power of pull marketing, a programmatic approach must be employed where every presentation delivered by the firm's employees is crafted in a manner that communicates a consistent message in the marketplace. That message must clearly differentiate your firm from competitors and be focused on the benefits clients will realize by engaging your firm, rather than touting the features of your firm. This is contrary to the approach used by most firms. Differentiating your firm from competitors can be accomplished two ways: analytically using 3-dimensional, attribute, or force field analysis; and operationally by developing and implementing unique operational methods that yield real performance improvements for both your client and your firm. Performance improvements developed in this manner are long-lasting, difficult for competitors to detect, and even more difficult for them to replicate. Moreover, this type of operational improvement can yield real results: improving client satisfaction and increasing your firm's profitability.

Second, the presentations must address burning issues important to client decision-makers rather than addressing legal matters, and they must be delivered at venues populated by client decision makers, not peers and competitors. If you wish to present at conferences, you must generally submit one or two topics for consideration as much as 6–12 months in advance and then hope to get selected. The application package typically requires information regarding the presenter such as their biography, a photograph, and a video sample of them presenting, as well as a description of the proposed content, learning objectives, and references who are familiar with your presentation skills. However, since COVID-19 drove greater acceptance of videoconferencing and improvements in the quality and performance of videoconferencing platforms, you can now take complete control of your firm's pull marketing initiative by creating and broadcasting content using Teams, Zoom, or similar software platforms, and specifically target audiences you choose to invite. This is an extremely low-cost way to reach a large number of high-potential prospects. By presenting in this manner, every prospect who attends now knows who you are, you have established yourself as a subject matter expert, you have offered potential solutions to what they perceive as pressing problems, and at the end of your presentation a magical thing happens. A few people approach you to talk more about the topic, and in doing so they have identified themselves as your warm leads. You must still close the deal, but this dramatically reduces the time and cost (less indirect labor and less travel and entertainment expenses) required to identify who needs your services and convince them of your suitability to help them. Contrast this with attending conferences and other events and attempting to network at receptions in an environment where it's difficult to talk with more than three or four people before it gets too noisy or people have too much to drink to hold a meaningful conversation, and where the odds of meeting the three or four people out of that crowd who need your services are astronomically low.

Third, while pull marketing provides a great opportunity to attract prospective clients to your firm by showcasing your subject matter expertise in concert with your communication and presentation skills, it's also an opportunity to drive clients away if your communication and presentation skills are less than ideal. Clients—especially large corporate or public clients—tend to want attorneys who are articulate, polished, and can express complex concepts and challenging processes in simple, concise terms. Yet, many attorneys, while they have tremendous legal knowledge and expertise, lack the knowledge and skills required to develop and deliver a superior presentation that leverages the power of the science of persuasive communication, and as a result deliver ineffective, mind-numbing presentations. The scientific principles mentioned above include things such as:

- Completely avoiding the use of text on slides;
- Carefully choosing images that will trigger an emotional response aligned with the desired outcome ten times faster than the human cognitive process;
- Changing slides at the right frequency to improve the relative concentration of the audience's brainwaves associated with attention, concentration, and relaxation;
- Focusing first on benefits the client will realize rather than the features characteristic of your firm or your approach;
- Aligning those benefits with the three factors that drive all decision making, which are gaining status or extreme economic benefit, what's good for people, and meeting requirements, and doing so in the order that is most likely to result in desired outcomes;
- Linking the benefits to the enabling features with a trigger word that initiates the pre-programmed human behavior of accepting what you say.

Note that these scientific principles are equally effective in negotiations and litigation.

Additionally, it's important not to confuse the concepts of practice and performance, meaning that you must devote sufficient time to practicing your presentation prior to its delivery. Otherwise, your performance becomes the practice, and you exhibit a low-quality characteristic of a practice session, resulting not only in low effectiveness, but in creating a lasting, unfavorable impression in the minds of the audience.

Push Marketing

Push marketing gets its name from the fact that it involves pushing yourself on a client by contacting them, requesting an appointment, and over time trying to build a relationship with them that can be leveraged into a revenue-generating situation. The term Push Marketing has a negative connotation. This is likely in part due to the associated image of pushing yourself on a client and the fact that many attorneys find it distasteful and anxiety-producing to make cold calls, but also due to the fact that prior to the 1977 Supreme Court decision (*Bates v. State Bar of Arizona* 433 U.S. 350) that attorney advertising was a form of commercial speech protected by the First Amendment, it was considered unethical to advertise or "sell" professional services. As an artifact of this issue, many attorneys and support personnel incorrectly use the terms marketing and business development because they are uncomfortable using the word sales. For the record, the term business development is an umbrella term that covers everything you do from beginning to end to bring work into the firm. It comprises two components: marketing and sales. Marketing is everything you do to help bring in work that is not related to a specific opportunity. So, things like your firm's website, attending conferences, and client meetings that are not related to a specific opportunity are marketing. Sales comprises all activities directed at winning a specific opportunity. This means that preparing a proposal or presentation specific to an opportunity is sales, as is a client meeting directed specifically at winning a discrete opportunity. Clearly, the terminology is misused within the industry. But the sooner you embrace the fact that your attorneys are tasked with performing sales activities, the sooner you can learn and apply sales techniques proven to produce superior results.

The success of push marketing is governed by a simple mathematical equation: $S = eF$, where S is the dollar volume of sales you generate, e is your effectiveness, and F is the amount of face time you have with prospective clients. Face-to-face time is defined as one-on-one time you have in an appointment with a prospect. Running into a prospect at a conference, for example, does not count as face-to-face time. Neither do two or three of your attorneys simultaneously meeting with a prospective client contact. Building a relationship with a prospective client is a lot like dating. If you were to take a third person on your date, you wouldn't be able to build much of a relationship with the person you were dating. Face time is finite, and often difficult to obtain. Thus, the key to achieving a large dollar volume of sales when using push marketing is your effectiveness. Yet, few attorneys have been trained in effective sales techniques. So, if you intend to rely on push marketing to grow your firm, it's a good idea to improve your attorneys' effectiveness by training them in sales techniques that are based on science and proven to work in the professional services industry.

While there are many proven sales techniques that can be applied synergistically, the most important technique is what I call the Colombo approach. Colombo is a television show in which Peter Falk played Detective Colombo. He gave the impression of being disheveled, bungling, and not very smart, yet he was brilliant. He would ask question after question, requesting help and information until he was able to piece together the solution. This same approach is very effective for gathering intelligence from prospective clients in a way that can help you to ultimately sell them your services by not selling your services. It is the yin and yang of sales that more frequently produces desired outcomes. The odds of you obtaining a signed contract during your first visit with a prospective client are low, so focus on gathering intelligence about the prospect and not on selling your services. When it's time for you to sell your services, they will let you know.

Many attorneys believe that making the cold call to get the first appointment is the most challenging aspect of push marketing. Until, of course, they get the first appointment, then they realize that obtaining subsequent appointments can be even more challenging because the prospect has already met with you. Why would they want to meet with you again? Many attorneys find this challenging only because they don't know what to do during the first appointment that makes a prospective client want them to return. The secret to being invited back is not providing free services, it's providing a small amount of very valuable information each time you meet with the prospect—information that will help the prospect look good to their boss, customers, or constituents, and help them further their career. This small act causes them to value your presence. In fact, when I meet with a prospect, or even an existing client, the second or third time I often receive the same compliment, and invitation, almost word for word. When I stand up to shake their hand and leave, the prospect or existing client says, "I should really meet with you more often because every time I do, I learn something new." When a prospect comes to this realization, you are likely to receive a contract shortly thereafter, and when voiced by an existing client, it's an indication that you're in a very good position to cross-sell that client additional types of services your firm offers, thereby strengthening your relationship while increasing your revenue and profitability. Clients who want you hanging around them are likely to be willing to pay higher rates for your presence because you have now differentiated yourself and your firm from competitors, and they feel that you are the only one who can provide what they need most.

Referrals

In a manner somewhat similar to Pull Marketing, Referrals, in comparison to Push Marketing, can significantly increase your likelihood of obtaining a contract from a prospect, reduce the lag time between your initial contact with the prospect and obtaining a contract, and correspondingly reduce your cost (indirect labor and travel and entertainment expenses) associated with business development. This is because when an existing client introduces you to a prospect it's an implied endorsement. The prospect you're being introduced to will typically assume that the person introducing you to them wouldn't be doing so unless they regard you highly and perceive that you provide them with services that are good value. This immediately helps you overcome the typical hesitation a prospect exhibits when considering engaging your firm for the first time. A prerequisite to obtaining a referral is providing outstanding service and good results for your existing client, noting that the service element is just as important as the results. For example, if you're assisting your client with a matter that takes six months to resolve, the client's experience interacting with you during that six months will significantly influence their perception of the value you provide regardless of the final outcome, and it will significantly impact their willingness to introduce you to other prospects because they don't want the referral to create backlash. In some cases, your clients can be your best salespersons, providing referrals without you needing to ask for them. But in many cases, you must specifically request an introduction for it to take place because providing such an introduction may simply not occur to the client.

Although many other methods exist for business development, within the organizational client sector the effectiveness of other methods pales in comparison to the three approaches described above and those other methods will likely result in a low return on your investment of time and money.

Expanding Your Client Base within the Individual Consumer Market Sector

The individual consumer market sector is highly segmented by characteristics such as gender, race, age, ethnicity, culture, and income, so it's prudent to carefully focus your business development efforts on segments that exhibit the best response rate and are most lucrative. This necessitates that you establish a system of metrics and track and analyze the return on investment you receive by type of service and market segment, and the various combinations and permutations of the two.

Prospects and revenue sources are highly decentralized within this market sector, so your success will depend even more on pull marketing than push marketing as compared with the organizational sector. Similarly, while all business development is governed by statistics, within the individual consumer market sector the response rate is typically very low, so reaching a large number of prospects is very important, as is the effectiveness of your messaging, which will strongly influence your return on investment.

There are nine factors that have the largest impact on the effectiveness of your messaging, as follows:

Differentiation

For good results, differentiate your firm from competitors by uniquely positioning it in the marketplace relative to other firms (e.g., high-end vs economy, local vs expert from afar, specialty firm vs jack of all trades). Effective differentiation is achieved by using a combination of two methods. The first method is analytical, with the three most effective analytical tools being 3-dimensional positioning analysis, attribute analysis, and force field analysis. When used in the consumer products industry these analyses can be time consuming, expensive, require lots of data, and necessitate the use of higher mathematics. However, in the legal industry few people are aware of these analytical tools and even fewer know how to use them properly, so you can use these tools to perform the differentiation analysis rapidly, inexpensively, with little data, and with rudimentary mathematics and yield very effective results. The second method for differentiating your firm from competitors is operationally. This involves the development and implementation of operating processes that are uncommon within the legal industry and result in more favorable results for your clients and your firm. Such operational improvements are very difficult for your competitors to detect and even harder for them to replicate, thereby providing a long-lasting competitive advantage.

Consistency

Once you've truly differentiated your firm it's important to use consistent messaging in the marketplace. This applies to all messaging such as that presented on your website, and in your social media posts, advertisements, elevator speech, and even your conversations with prospects and existing clients. Moreover, all aspects of your firm, from the appearance of your offices, attorneys, and staff, to your behaviors, must be consistent with your differentiated message.

Frequency

When your clientele is derived from the individual consumer sector, owning the prospect's mind share is critical to achieving your full business development potential. Owning mind share means that when the prospect needs a service your firm provides, your firm is the one they think of first. This comes from frequent contact with the prospect to reinforce name recognition and exhibiting a readily accessible presence as close to the time of need as possible. Obtaining mind share ownership requires a carefully crafted approach because of a scientific phenomenon called the mere exposure effect. This is the tendency of people to develop a preference for a concept, such as the idea of hiring your firm, the more they are exposed to it. However, to have the desired effect the repetition must be very subtle. If the message is repeated overtly, it has the opposite of the desired outcome, and the prospective client is less likely to want to hire your firm. You have probably experienced this kind of adverse reaction yourself when you've been exposed to the overt repetition of an advertisement over and over again.

Unaided Recall

Regardless of the frequency of your communication with prospects, the odds of you being in contact with them at the exact instant they need your services are very low. This means that their unaided recall of your firm's message, meaning how well they remember it without any assistance or another reminder, is critical to obtaining their business. Unaided recall is enhanced by communicating in a manner that leverages the full power of their cognitive process. Although humans have an almost unlimited memory capacity, our cognitive capabilities are very limited. When we see words on a screen and hear the same or similar information presented verbally, our brain is simultaneously receiving information through two different pathways—our vision and our hearing. This causes us to subconsciously compare the two inputs to determine whether they are the same, and this act of comparing the information consumes most of our cognitive resources, making it difficult for us to process and store information in our memory, reducing our capability for unaided recall of the information. This is why people often hear me use the phrase "Bullets kill presentations," and why training programs that incorporate slides with bullet points are less effective than those that don't. Thus, to improve unaided recall of your firm's name in the minds of prospective and existing clients, you must carefully control how your message is communicated.

Primacy Effect

The primacy effect is a term used to describe a type of human cognitive bias where a person tends to remember the first part of the information you convey in your communications more than other parts. To leverage the power of this natural behavior, in your messaging you must convey the most important aspects first.

Recency Effect

The recency effect refers to the psychological phenomenon that most people remember the last piece of information you convey to them with the greatest accuracy. Thus, to leverage this effect, you must subtly repeat the initial, most important aspects of your message again at the end of your communication.

Repetition

Many marketing professionals rely on what is called the Rule of Seven, meaning that a person needs to see an advertisement seven times before they will be likely to act on it. This concept was originally conceived in the 1930s and was in 1956 demonstrated to have some scientific validity, although the number of repetitions was shown to be in the range of five to nine. Many people believe that the Rule of Seven still applies, but in today's world, where your cell phone and other devices listen to your conversations and send you related advertisements, and we have increased exposure to advertisements through an intensive stream of digital posts, unsolicited emails, unwanted robocalls, and other invasions of our lives, many people have little patience for repetitive advertising that can be characterized as intrusive. So, more creative and powerful messaging becomes more important as a means for achieving desired results with less frequency.

Imagery

When a person sees a photographic image, it triggers an emotional response approximately ten times faster than the human cognitive process. And, once this emotional response has been triggered, that person's perception is polarized like a magnet and difficult to change. People will go to great lengths to justify their initial impression regardless of any subsequently provided evidence to the contrary. Thus, images are a powerful tool for achieving your desired outcomes, but they must be carefully selected so that the perceptions you create with those images are well aligned with your desired outcomes.

Visualization

Long ago, history used to be taught by telling stories. It's also effective as a sales tool because it enables the audience to visualize themselves using your services, gives them comfort of reduced risk because it illustrates that others like them have used your firm's services, and it's a powerful mnemonic tool.

Today, you have a wide range of tools that you can choose from to communicate your message to prospective clients. They vary greatly in cost from those that are very inexpensive, such as social media platforms, to more moderately priced print media, and more expensive media such as movie theaters, billboards, radio, and television. Choosing the right tool is a function of your desired clientele's characteristics. To gather data to support choosing an effective communication tool, you can survey your most valuable existing clients and ask them questions such as: do they use social media, and if so, which platforms? Do they live locally, and if so, do they listen to the radio when driving or pay attention to billboards? If they listen to the radio, ask what stations they tune in to and what roads they travel on most frequently. And, perhaps most importantly, how did they come to find out about your firm?

In addition to the data you collect in this manner, you will find that each media organization has a sales staff who can share data with you concerning the demographics of people they reach. Combining the information from your own surveys and that provided by the media organizations will help you make an educated decision as to where you should be advertising to reach your intended audience. While the temptation is great to rely heavily on social media because of its low cost, trendy nature, and broad reach, if your typical client doesn't use social media, it's not likely to bring you many new clients. Leveraging the power of science with data driven advertising generally produces the best return on investment.

Branding

The concept of branding as a means for differentiation has been in existence for thousands of years, but its use in marketing in a form similar to what we see today did not take shape until around the 1940s, and it was associated primarily with selling products. Because it was considered unethical to advertise professional services until the late 1970s, branding professional services is a relatively new concept and it's often misunderstood and misapplied. Many professional services firms engaged in law, architecture, engineering, accounting, and health care have launched branding and rebranding initiatives focused on logos, colors, and slogans, without analytically defining a differentiated market position, which is key to establishing your brand identity. But more importantly, for all but the most notable law firms, branding is largely ineffective because brand is not very often one of the key decision factors in selecting a firm. Branding is most effective for products that are status oriented, and where the brand is highly visible. For instance, people notice whether you drive a Lamborghini, Mercedes, or Ford, whether you wear a Rolex or a Timex, and whether you wear an Armani or Stafford (JC Penney) suit. But for many products that are not status oriented, such as Coca-Cola, branding is not very effective. You can see a Coca-Cola advertisement 20 times, but if you like the taste of Pepsi, when it's time to buy a soda, you'll buy a Pepsi. So, unless you're a high-profile firm, branding is not likely to bring in much revenue for you. And, if you are a high-profile firm, you will earn a greater return on investment if your branding initiative focuses on clearly defining a differentiated market position.

Chapter 4
Attorney Recruiting and Retention

Chuck Roberts

The Power of Superior Recruiting and Retention Practices

You can significantly improve your firm's revenue, profitability, and image, enhance the alignment, engagement, morale, and productivity of your employees, and reduce the time and attention required of your firm's leaders to supervise employees when you implement best practices for recruiting and retention. Additionally, these best practices can provide a significant competitive advantage for your firm because few firms are fully aware of these practices, and seldom implement them with consistency and discipline. A primary root cause for the failure to implement them with consistency and discipline is that many law firms don't recognize or acknowledge the full impact that recruiting and retention has on law firm operations and the effect that operational practices have on your ability to achieve desired legal outcomes for your clients. So, they don't give these practices the attention they deserve.

When presented with best practices, many law firm leaders immediately say, "We don't have time for that!" or "That would be very costly!" What they don't realize is that they are spending more time and money now by applying less-effective practices. They simply don't see the aggregated cost of their current practices because many of the cost components aren't easily recognized or quantified. For example, it's easy to calculate the readily apparent costs of lost revenue experienced during the time between when an attorney leaves and their replacement arrives, the cost incurred from having to pay a headhunter fee to find a candidate, and the signing bonus and relocation costs to bring a new person on board. But those costs often pale in comparison to those that are more difficult to quantify, such as your firm's lost revenue and profit when a client follows a departing attorney; the damage done to your client relationships and ability to achieve desired outcomes resulting from a departing attorney not being focused on their engagement for the six to nine months prior to their departure when they were searching for another job; the cost of training and mentoring that you performed to elevate the capabilities and qualifications of the person who is walking out the door; and the damage to your firm's reputation when word on the street is that attorneys are leaving your firm. And this is not a comprehensive list.

The proper way to view the implementation of best recruiting and retention practices is that you will stop *spending* on your current approach and start *investing* in a superior approach that will provide a return on that investment.

The Seven Keys to Superior Recruiting

Although many factors can influence the success of your recruiting efforts, the following seven items typically have a greater impact than all other factors combined. These items are synergistic, meaning that when used together the impact of each item is greater than if used individually.

Focus Your Sourcing

Until you take the steps described in the remainder of this chapter to make your firm a magnet for top talent, you'll find that the best candidates are usually those who aren't looking to change employers. This means that direct recruiting (i.e., identifying who you would like to hire and then calling them) is your best approach for recruiting the most talented people. And there are three easy ways to find these people. The first method is searching your competitors' websites and identifying those personnel who have the capabilities and experience you seek; the second method is identifying candidates who impress you when serving in the role of opposing counsel; and the third method is identifying by word of mouth who is viewed as a top-notch attorney. Star performers often work as part of a team with other high-performance attorneys and support personnel, so when you connect with a star, it's wise to consider the potential for a lift-out of the entire team. Other methods for sourcing candidates, such as networking, using LinkedIn, and posting advertisements are far less likely to produce top quality candidates. When sourcing candidates, prepare a list of the three to five most important attributes you seek in a candidate, and consider no more than those attributes. Firms that develop a long list of job qualifications reduce their likelihood of finding a suitable candidate, and reduce their ability to select a candidate who will be successful at the most critical aspects of the position.

Have an Executive Make the Initial Contact

While it's tempting to have an internal or external recruiter or others in your firm's human resources department perform the sourcing step and make initial contact with the prospective candidate, you're more likely to obtain a response, and receive a more favorable response, when an executive of your firm who is knowledgeable about the candidate's attributes makes the initial contact by telephone. This is especially true in a tight labor market where prospective candidates are bombarded by emails and calls from recruiters and after receiving many contacts of this nature become irritated and unresponsive. A telephone call from your firm's managing partner demonstrates to the candidate that you think they are important. When contact is made, you can increase the likelihood the candidate will respond affirmatively by applying the science of persuasive communication. The six primary persuasive communication principles to use in this situation are:

- Communicating a single message that differentiates your firm from others;
- Keeping the conversation focused on the candidate instead of your firm;
- Presenting the benefits the candidate will experience from joining your firm;
- Aligning those benefits with the three factors that drive all decision making (i.e., gaining status or extreme economic benefit, what's good for people, and meeting requirements, in that order);
- Following the aligned benefits with a trigger word such as because (this increases the likelihood the candidate will accept what you've said);
- Following the trigger word with the features of your firm that enable and correspond to the cited benefits.

This approach is the exact opposite of the manner in which more than 99.9% of all people communicate, and can itself be a powerful differentiator.

Be Rigorous and Decisive

In today's busy world, there's a tendency to keep interviews short and have firm leaders, in particular, limit the time they spend with a candidate. Some leaders will say they can tell right away whether someone is a good fit. This is characteristic of firms that make costly hiring mistakes. Best practices call for an all-day, challenging interview where multiple people in various practices, departments, and levels interview the candidate and each ask many of the same questions. Using this approach, you'll see the candidate when they are fresh and energetic, and when they are tired and worn down. As you approach the end of the day, convene the group of people who have interviewed the candidate and compare the responses each of you received to each question, share impressions, and make a decision as to whether you will hire them. Be picky about who you choose to hire and create the buzz that it's difficult to get hired by your firm. Creating an air of exclusivity will attract top talent. If the candidate is one you would like to hire, have the managing partner or another high-level executive of your firm present the offer to the candidate before they leave your office, giving them a reasonable period of time (such as seven to ten days) to make a decision. Your firm's decisiveness and prompt action will favorably impress the candidate and start the clock ticking on their decision period, thereby limiting the candidate's ability to shop around for other offers. Firms that drag out the decision to make an offer cause the candidate to think the firm is bureaucratic, doesn't have enough work to support hiring them, is disinterested, or is disorganized, none of which bode well for the candidate accepting your offer.

Emphasize Total Compensation

When presenting a candidate with an offer, your likelihood of obtaining their acceptance is enhanced by providing them a one-page document that presents their total compensation and itemizes the various components, showing how the dollar value of each component contributes to the total. Include base pay, medical, dental, and vision care, flexible spending account, life insurance, short- and long-term care, child care, paid time off, profit sharing, 401(k) contributions, continuing education, vehicle allowance, and any other elements of value.

Make the Decision Easier

A decision to change employers is typically difficult and involves many considerations, but when it involves relocation, the decision is vastly more stressful and complex. You can make it easier for those candidates who will have to relocate by providing them with a single source for obtaining information critical to their decision process. In doing so, you will also show the candidate that you value their time and understand what's important to them. This is achieved by preparing a page on your website corresponding to each of your office locations that provides the following information:

- *A general description of the location.* Describe the office's proximity to major highways and airports (recognizing they may need to travel back to their prior location). Include information about the major amenities proximal to the office. Emphasize that working at your office places them in an environment that will make their time off enjoyable and convenient.
- *A description of the office.* Include a description of the building, office space, work environment, and support staff. Include photographs of the building, office interior, and people in your office collaborating on engagements.
- *A description of the area.* Include the size and characteristics of the city and county. In this section include a map illustrating the office location relative to the major highways and airport mentioned earlier.
- *A list of local recreation and entertainment options.* Prepare a very diverse list to appeal to a wide array of interests and include items such as major shopping centers, golf courses, performing arts centers, sports stadiums, the zoo, and other unique attributes of the specific area such as equestrian facilities, the beach or lakes, amusement parks, and auto, motorcycle, or bicycle race tracks.
- *Information regarding the K-12 school system.* Include the number of schools of each type, graduation rate, the number of students, teachers, and employees, and the capital budget. Include a hyperlink to a report that shows the academic ranking of each school in the district, and provide a link to information about the District's International Baccalaureate (IB) program. Include information regarding private K-12 schools available within the county.
- *A list of higher education facilities within a 50-mile radius.* Include the facility's name, location, whether they are public or private, and whether they offer 2- or 4-year programs.

- *A list of hospitals located within the county.* Include the hospital name, number of beds, and trauma level designation.
- *Information about the local economy.* Include the local unemployment rate, anticipated job growth over the next ten years, and top seven occupational categories in the county, ranked by percentage of the population engaged in the listed occupations.
- *Information about the local crime rate.* List the 20 cities in the United States with the highest murder rates (murders per 100,000 people). Indicate where your office location falls relative to this list. If your office is located in a city that's in the top 20 for crime, still list this information because it's likely the candidate will look it up anyway, and it's best you don't appear to be hiding anything. If your office is in a city in the top 20 but the neighborhood in which the office is located has a crime rate lower than the aggregate rate for the city, show that level of detail.

Act on Feedback

Whether a candidate accepts or declines an offer, request a debriefing about their experience interacting with your firm during the hiring process from the initial contact through the offer and any ensuing negotiations. Candidates are not likely to reveal everything they think and feel and may provide misleading information to avoid an awkward situation or burning a bridge. However, if you compare the intelligence gathered from debriefing multiple candidates you can usually identify patterns that indicate procedural flaws you can address to improve your hiring process and achieve a higher success rate. Remember that candidate perceptions are their reality, and that your perception on such issues doesn't matter.

Turn New Hires into Recruiters

New hires frequently communicate with their peers about their first day on the job. If their first day is consumed by filling out redundant on-boarding forms and sitting in an office reading the employee manual and descriptions of your firm's prior engagements, and their office is not properly prepared and fully equipped for them when they arrive, they are likely to broadcast an unfavorable review of their first day on the job, and once that impression is made it's difficult to change it despite what subsequent days may bring. Conversely, if you implement on-boarding procedures that eliminate redundancy, provide the new hire with forms that are already populated with as much data as possible and require little more than their signature, have their desk, computer, email, and other office tools set up for them, and immediately get the new hire actively engaged participating in planning meetings and cases, their communications with peers are more likely to be characterized by excitement and describe the tremendous opportunities they have accessed by joining your firm, making their peers interested in joining.

The Seven Keys to Superior Retention

To identify what led to an attorney's resignation, many firms will conduct an exit interview. Such interviews seldom produce useful or actionable information because exiting personnel typically filter their comments and in many cases are unable to identify or articulate the actual root causes for their feelings. Research has revealed there are seven keys to superior retention. They correspond one-to-one with the top seven real reasons for voluntary resignation, and are all within the control of an attorney's supervisor. Keep in mind that you may not agree with an attorney's perception of conditions at your firm, but to them, their perception is their reality. So, if you want to improve retention, you must acknowledge and address these perceptions as being real.

Provide a Challenge

Continuous growth and development are key to a professional's sense of worth, especially for those attorneys who are your top performers. If they feel they are always delegated the same type of engagements, aren't progressing with respect to their role on engagements, and aren't given increasing autonomy, they will be inclined to seek greater responsibility elsewhere. It's especially easy for a supervisor to fall into the trap of assigning an engagement to an attorney who has performed well on a similar engagement without regard to the attorney's level of interest in a similar engagement. Have supervisors train their successor and prepare their other subordinates for advancement to other areas of the firm. Unfortunately, some supervisors instead act selfishly, trying to keep the best attorneys on their own team and consciously or unconsciously create situations that preclude advancement. The best practice is for the supervisor to have a regular dialogue with each of their subordinates regarding their career interests and provide an array of engagements that will support the attorney's growth and development along a path that aligns with their interests and goals. A review of prior engagements assigned to each subordinate is instrumental in identifying existing conditions that need to be promptly addressed before the attorney leaves.

Create Confidence in the Firm's Leadership

Attorneys spend a lot of their time working and want to feel that those efforts are not in vain. If they detect flaws in the firm's governance or leadership, they're likely to move to a firm they believe is more likely to successfully capitalize on their efforts. Often a supervisor will become close to their subordinates and share too much information, or the wrong type of information, with personnel. When such information includes judgmental or derogatory comments regarding one or more of the firm's leaders it can degrade the employee's confidence in the firm's leadership, and once this occurs the process is difficult to reverse. Supervisors by virtue of their role in the firm are an extension of the leadership team and their expression of support for leadership decisions and actions, whether or not they personally have a different opinion, is critical to retention. Opposing views should be expressed directly to leaders in private leadership meetings, and when those meetings are adjourned, everyone must act as a team and accept and overtly support decisions that were made. It's best practice for supervisors to look for opportunities to call attention to positive aspects of the firm's leadership.

Foster a Positive Professional Relationship with Subordinates

The supervisor serves as the face of the company for their subordinates. Thus, it's critical that the supervisor be perceived as fair and consistent, having integrity, and possessing a genuine concern regarding the attorney as a person. At the same time, that supervisor must appropriately delegate responsibility and authority, and hold their subordinates accountable for performance, all while providing support as needed, and being empathetic, not sympathetic. It's a complex role. Yet few attorneys have received any formal training in supervisory techniques. Years of experience as a successful attorney is not a substitute for supervisory skills. The best practice to address this issue is providing supervisory skills training for all existing supervisors (including the firm's executives) and future supervisors, and, recognizing that training is a process not an event, providing follow-up coaching for each supervisor until they're capable of successfully applying those skills in a wide array of circumstances. This approach will provide a significant return on investment in the form of higher morale, increased productivity, less conflict, greater retention, and lower risk exposure to employee claims.

Provide Recognition

A good supervisor knows that they could not have achieved their accomplishments without the contributions of their subordinates, so being humble and very publicly giving credit to subordinates where credit is due is very important to employee satisfaction and retention. Supervisors who do this will find that attorneys are eager to work for them because those attorneys know their efforts will be rewarded. The most effective recognition and rewards are often not monetary.

Facilitate Work/Life Balance

The concept of work/life balance is widely misunderstood in the context of retention. Many supervisors think it means that attorneys don't want to work a lot of overtime, but research has revealed that it's more directly related to fairness, and a supervisor's ability and willingness to promptly address issues of nonperformance. For example, if the firm is engaged by a new, strategically important client, the supervisor will assign that engagement to their best performing subordinate. If an engagement with another important client is landed by the firm, the supervisor won't want to trust that to a poor performer, so they will again assign it to their top performer. This sort of practice continues until the top performer is burdened with a very demanding workload, and the poor performer is coasting on easy engagements that require less effort and overtime. The top performer sees the disparity and begins to feel resentment for having to work so hard and so many hours, and wonders why the supervisor won't hold the poor performer accountable or get rid of them. Left unaddressed, the resentment leads to the top performer's lack of respect for the supervisor, dissatisfaction with the work environment, and resignation. High-performance attorneys love accountability. Low performance attorneys hate it.

Communicate Differently

If you were to ask Human Resource directors what item employees most frequently cite as being in need of improvement, an overwhelming majority would say that item is communication. Firms that recognize this issue often try to communicate more frequently, more inclusively, and be more transparent, but these approaches seldom work. That's because more than 99.9% of all people think, write, and speak backward from the most effective approach, and doing more of a thing that's being done ineffectively does not solve the problem. Poor communication reduces the effectiveness and return on investment in your firm's business development and adversely impacts your ability to win cases, but in a human resources context it leads to reduced alignment, engagement, productivity, and morale, and ultimately has an adverse impact on retention. To correct this issue, apply scientific principles of communication. In this application the principles with the greatest impact are those described under the *Have an Executive Make the Initial Contact* header of the Recruiting section of this chapter.

Accommodate Perceptions of Value

Attorneys assign value to aspects of their employment with your firm, including conventional elements of compensation, based on their personal circumstances. In some cases, factors related to their employment not addressed by the conventional elements of compensation may be of great importance to them, and they may not take the initiative to advise you of those factors until you receive their resignation. The best practice to avoid this type of surprise is for the supervisor to have regular, periodic dialogue with each of their subordinates directed at understanding what's important to the attorney and when an attorney's needs fall outside the realm of conventional compensation. When this issue is detected, initiate discussions with your firm's leadership and human resources department to determine if there is a way to accommodate those needs. When the firm is responsive to individual needs in this manner it often creates a strong bond between the attorney and the firm that dramatically strengthens retention.

Chapter 5

Meaningful Lawyer Development as a Tool for Success

Sandra J. Boyer

As a high school and college athlete, I grew up accustomed to consistent training and performance as essentialities in developing the skills, experience, and endurance I needed to achieve my goals. The expectation for learning, maintaining, and excelling in sport is not much different than the expectations set forth for young lawyers. In the same way that I recognized these expectations as a young athlete, I don't think the expectations of young lawyers is a surprise to them. What they may find surprising, however—as I did during my years as an upper classman—is that personal discipline and determination may push an individual athlete forward, but there is no guarantee that it will sustain the team's performance. Support and mentoring from the upper classmen and coaches was the guiding force for team success, and therefore, a guiding force in my success.

Building, developing, and supporting the team of a law firm is much the same as guiding and growing a track team. As leaders, you must determine what your team needs for success, recruit performers who can meet those needs, and then train, mentor, and support those professionals for their success and the success of the team. Picture a relay team: four runners, each positioned for and responsible for only one leg of the race. Their individual performance and success are being relied upon by the rest of the team; however, a relay rarely finds success if each leg of the race is not equally accounted and planned for by the coach. As each runner progresses in his or her performance, the team's collective speed increases; however, the team's time may be affected by faults in the exchange zone, or the team may be disqualified if their hand-offs resulted in a dropped baton. That being the case, many coaches rely on the upper classmen to run the second and fourth legs of the race—braiding in the experienced talent among the new runners—mentoring.

Successful steps for the development of young lawyers include (1) effective recruitment, (2) organized orientation, (3) structured training, and (4) focused retention efforts. Chapter 3 discussed effective recruitment and focused retention strategies. In this chapter we will discuss organized orientation and structured training. Mentoring of new lawyers and the roles that current law firm members play in guiding the team toward building a successful firm will also be highlighted as a key component of training.

New Lawyer Orientation Programs

After making the initial investment in recruiting new lawyers, it is time to ensure that return on the firm's investment. Stewarding the firm's time, money, and capacity when it comes to identifying and recruiting lawyers who can be successful in the firm also includes coaching new hires in the firm's culture. On-boarding those new lawyers with a structured orientation program bridges the gap between "new" lawyer and "member" of the firm. Back to our analogy, think of it as training camp. We've brought in a new bunch of athletes, now it is time to get them unpacked and settled in.

An innovative orientation program, developed appropriately and implemented consistently, will increase the ability of new lawyers to begin their race from a solid set of blocks. The firm's dedication to a strong orientation program demonstrates a commitment to the lawyer's success as an individual as well as part of the firm team. It provides an opportunity for people within the firm to meet and get to know the new hires. This begins to build confidence within the new lawyer and confidence within the team.

Elements of a New Lawyer Orientation Program

Implementing a unified and structured orientation program provides a welcoming, inclusive atmosphere, and an impactful first impression. The program intentionally provides new lawyers with what is necessary to become functional quickly, a roster of individuals and their functions within the firm, all firm expectations, and answers questions honestly as they arise.

Organized orientation may be delineated into modules that overview:

- Firm leadership and administration
- Standards of professional conduct
- Firm financials and processes
- Lawyer and career development
- Client development

The program may be structured in a way where new lawyers may gradually learn about the firm over a several week period—preventing them from becoming overwhelmed and allowing for some self-paced work.

Administrative and Firm Overview

For instance, week one may feature legal administrators and managing partners welcoming new lawyers in a traditional orientation style.

The legal administrator or office manager may begin with a scheduled in-person office tour, introducing new lawyers to members of the firm. Pro-active communication about when this tour will be happening and how it will be led is important information to share with current firm members, so they are prepared to receive and meet their new colleagues.

In conjunction with the tour, provide an on-boarding session that includes:

- a discussion of salary and benefit information;
- an introduction to the assigned support personnel and process for utilization;
- a discussion and written description of firm policies and procedures, timekeeping, calendaring and docket control, client management system, etc. for reference;
- a calendar of firm social functions;
- an introduction to and demonstration of the firm's technology systems;

- a review of the firm's CLE process; and
- other important matters specific to the firm.

The managing partner may meet with the new lawyers following their tour and on-boarding session to discuss:

- the history of the firm;
- the vision, mission, and core values;
- how firm culture is based on these values;
- the associate assessment and evaluation process;
- the associate training and mentoring program;
- an introduction of the firm mentoring program and the assigned mentor;
- a description of firm management, including committees;
- billable hour expectations, billing receipt expectations;
- firm and individual lawyer client development efforts;
- who the lawyer should approach with questions or concerns;
- the path to partnership;
- firm practices and clients;
- billing procedures and the role they play; and
- ethics, confidentiality and firm expectations.

Professionalism Overview

Once the new lawyer has settled into the firm's physical environment, been on-boarded, and has had a chance to be introduced to the people of the firm, a review of the standards of professional behavior may be reviewed. Depending on the firm's orientation schedule, this may come three to four weeks into the new hire. This review should be conducted in a one-on-one format between the new lawyer and his or her assigned mentor or senior lawyer.

The conversation serves as a review of the rules of professional conduct and an opportunity for new lawyers to ask questions of their mentor in an individual rather than group setting. It is important for the firm to reiterate their vision, mission, core values and how these are relevant to the duties owed to clients, duties owed to an opposing party, duties owed to a witness, duty of candor owed to a court, how to recognize conflict, the lawyer's responsibility regarding non-lawyer assistants, and ethics issues such as client confidentiality and conflicts checks when accepting new clients. Part of creating a cohesive and successful team is understanding how behavior and conduct contribute to the overall firms' culture and its function—including the consequences of veering out of the lane of established expectations.

Financial Overview

For lawyers to become future leaders, they must be coached for success. Of course they need to obtain skills in the practice of law, but they also need to understand the business of the practice of law. An early engagement with firm finances may positively impact lawyer performance as it pertains to financial strategy. The financial overview can help new lawyers reach the finish line faster. While individual financial expectations have been shared through the firm overview, their information intake must also include firm financial knowledge. During their second month with the firm, the new lawyer may receive more detailed information on the business, such as:

- the firm's client intake procedure;
- the firm's retainer agreement and how it is used;
- the firm's billing procedures, including billing rates and alternative billing methods;
- financial reports, key performance indicators (KPIs), and how they are used as management tools;
- a description of the financial reports provided to associates, what the information means, and the expectations of financial performance;
- general firm financial management considerations such as, WIP, A/Rs, Billings, Collections and Budgeting (Expense vs. Income); and
- the role played by lawyers in meeting financial expectations.

The firm financial partner may be the best positioned to conduct the financial overview. If the firm lacks a formal partner in charge of finances, the managing partner or CFO may conduct the overview. Plan for all questions to be addressed, deliberately use language that can easily be understood by lawyers with no financial expertise and share as much information as is appropriate. This leads to a better understanding of the role they play in helping the firm meet its financial goals and the importance of accountability for timekeeping, billing, and collection.

Career Development Overview

After the new lawyer has been with the firm for several weeks and been educated on the firm's finances, it is appropriate for the firm to perform a career development overview. The assigned mentor, the professional personnel partner, or the managing partner may invite their mentee into a conversation about the importance of the roles of the new lawyer and the firm. This review should be an interactive review. The firm will share their expectations of the new lawyer including, performance, attendance, billing, client management, staff treatment, participation in associate events and firm events, client treatment and participation and adherence to firm core values and culture. The new lawyer should share with the firm their career goals, their legal skills growth plan, their practice interests, and time management philosophy. This review may be a key tool in opening communication, so both the firm and the lawyer get a sense of how to account for this new lawyer's leg of the relay.

Client Development Overview

Once the new lawyer has learned about the internal aspects of the firm and shared their goals with the firm, they will be ready to represent the firm outwardly in the community. Before they do so though, the client development overview should take place. In all previous overview meetings, the new lawyer will have been reminded that, while in public, they are acting as a representative of the firm. This overview will focus on developing relationships that can transition to work generation. The foundation for this overview will contain the firm client development and marketing philosophy, strategies, and events. It may also discuss client development activities including writing articles, LinkedIn, social events, branding, firm representation, how to generate more work from current clients, how to cross-market, speaking engagements, pro-bono work, contacting clients, referral sources, and so on. This session serves as a team huddle. It should leave the new lawyer feeling like they've just learned the firm chant, secret handshake, or ritual. Only the best example of a successful rainmaker who is passionate about client generation should be charged to lead this element of the orientation program.

A strong orientation program provides essential tools and supports for new lawyers to get out of the blocks quickly, have the stamina to stay in the race, and reach the finish line faster. Unfortunately, there is no winners' podium in orientation—so how do we know if the program is delivering on its performance promises?

Program Assessment and Evaluation

When assessing whether the orientation program was effective, ask, Do the new lawyers know:

- the firm's expectations?
- their ethical responsibilities?
- the resources available?
- how to use firm technology and systems?
- applicable aspects of the business of the practice of law?
- the amount of client interaction they will have early, later?
- the role the firm/new lawyer will play in their development?
- the path to partnership?
- how to develop clients?
- the firm vision, mission, core values, and culture?
- how to stay at the firm and be part of its success?

When evaluating your orientation program, ask the following:

- Do the new lawyers live up to firm expectations? Daily? Annually?
- Are they deemed ethical by their peers?
- What has been their utilization of firm resources?
- Do the effectively use firm technology and systems?
- Do they engage with the business of the practice of law? Or shy away?
- Is the amount of client interaction they have appropriate?
- Have they drafted a development plan? A path to partnership?
- Have they developed any clients? Participated in client development?
- Do they embody the firm vision, mission, core values, and culture? Do they represent this to the public?
- How have they bought into the firm's success?

Assessing the lawyers' retention and application of information shared during orientation can take place within the new lawyers first year. Was the new lawyer pro-active? Did they need a lot of handholding? Were they receptive to constructive feedback, and so on? Was the process helpful? Evaluating the program may be a long-term process whereby a lawyer's performance within the firm may help inform how the program may need to be altered or updated to ensure more effective outcomes for future participants.

New Lawyer Training Programs

Potential benefits of a structured lawyer training program are:

- Increases lawyer retention
- Helps lawyers be better faster
- Enhances client service
- Increases client retention
- Assists in client succession
- Assists with law firm management succession
- Provides financial benefits to the firm
- Assists with lawyer recruitment
- Enhances client generation

While these benefits may be universal, a lawyer training program will look different depending on the vision, mission, core values, and culture of each law firm. It is important to develop the program informed by the firm's diversity of practice, lawyer identities and personalities, and administrative resources of the firm.

A strong lawyer training program includes elements like:

- assigning a person(s) to be responsible for the training of lawyers;
- developing and using a primary task performance check list for each practice area;
- using that practice area checklist to evaluate the lawyer growth in the skills and qualification in that practice area;
- developing and implementing a CLE program (internal and external) focused on developing skills in substantive legal areas;
- developing and implementing a "training bank of hours" policy assisting the lawyers to learn without billable hours expectation for those hours;
- an evaluation program tracking the lawyer progress versus expectations of the firm;
- an organized mentoring program;
- the development and use of a personal business plan focusing on the career path of the new lawyer;
- an open communications process that keeps new lawyers informed about the business of the firm.

Today's post-COVID-19 world of work has evolved to include the use of flex time, working from a home office space, focusing on work/life balance, and lawyer movement from firm to firm. While it may be difficult for senior lawyers to be motivated to invest time in training younger lawyers due to this change in the field being foreign to them, firms will benefit from adjusting to this culture shift. New lawyers need to view their roles as helping to develop the firm and an individual career rather than just having a job. Senior lawyers need to make their investment in training known as an investment in firm and lawyer development, not just increased firm profits. Law firm success is dependent on the human resources they have, so focusing on the enhancement of the human experience is paramount in ensuring the persistence of the firm. One way of communicating the importance of a new lawyer and the importance of the firm team is to integrate a mentoring program into their training.

An Effective Lawyer Mentoring Program

Mentoring is a vital part of the new lawyer training program. A mentoring program may be formal or informal. Through the program, firms share the knowledge, skills, wisdom, and experience of the senior lawyers with the next generation of client service leaders. A strong mentoring program can serve as the conduit to do this.

Mentors are coaches. New team members observe and learn from them. If effective, mentors may be shadowed by mentees to facilitate growth and development in an organized and structured format. It helps firm lawyers enculturate young lawyers rather than simply push expectations upon them without support.

Benefits of a strong mentoring program far outweigh the time investment needed to make it successful. Mentoring may be full of joy and rewarding if approached with the right frame of mind. Consider what mentoring can do. It can:

- help new lawyers more effectively build a strong practice for long-term success;
- help new lawyers develop skills and abilities more quickly with focused oversight and feedback;
- develop a mentoring relationship between the mentor/mentee that builds loyalty between the firm and the new lawyer—commitment to their growth and development is demonstrated;
- provide new lawyers the opportunity to learn about leadership and how they can develop those skills;
- diminish frustration with the practice of law because there is a structured and organized process by which to answer questions and concerns;

- increase lawyer retention;
- effectively mentor lawyers to become quality firm lawyers at a higher percentage which attracts higher quality lawyers and clients;
- better mentor and train lawyers to become more profitable quicker;
- increase the number of qualified lawyers which enhances overall client service; and
- integrate lawyers into the firm faster and be more effective sooner, in practice and in other aspects of the firm as well.

The Role and Responsibilities of Mentors and Mentees

The Mentor

A pro-active mentor is a successful mentor. Serving as a mentor is a commitment to the firm, to the mentee, and to the client. The role includes helping develop a vision for the mentee that integrates firm expectations. It also requires the ability to listen and understand the aspirations and desires of the mentee and compare them to the firms.

The functional aspects of the role may be:

- assisting the mentee to transition from law school to associate;
- outlining firm expectations;
- new lawyer firm integration;
- new lawyer growth and development planning and implementation;
- assisting in the development of a personal business plan and then monitoring its implementation;
- acting as a sounding board;
- helping the new lawyer to develop leadership qualities;
- acting as a role model;
- identifying and helping hone client development skills; or
- helping the mentee to develop time management, timekeeping, client interaction, and other practice management skills.

The responsibilities might be:

- understanding the goals and objectives of the training program;
- ensuring the mentee is familiar with the orientation and reference manual, and the mentor program and process;
- creating a communications program and schedule for the relationship;
- ensuring the mentee meets others in the firm;

- spending time with the mentee in a variety of areas including lunch, client functions, substantive client work meetings, client meetings as appropriate, firm functions, etc.;
- encouraging the mentee to build collegiality with associates, partners, and staff;
- reviewing the workload of the mentee on a regular basis to ensure the type of work being delegated is appropriate and that the amount of work is feasible;
- providing regular feedback regarding performance of legal work as well as other areas of performance;
- answering questions and address concerns;
- acting as a confidant to the mentee while respecting confidentiality; or
- regularly submitting reports regarding the progress of the mentee.

The Mentee

Successful lawyers have many traits in common, but perhaps the most important trait is their ability to take responsibility for their own success. The mentee must understand that while they are assigned a mentor, the mentor is available to support them through their career development, not be responsible for it. The success of the mentoring program will largely depend on the initiative, dedication, and commitment demonstrated by the mentee.

The mentee must be willing to learn—keeping an ear to the coach's guidance—as well as able to take the baton and run with it—utilizing their training. The role of the mentee should be discussed and outlined before the relationship moves forward.

Depending on firm culture, their role might be described as:

- demonstrating a willingness to learn from the mentor and others in the firm;
- thinking through assignments, delegating projects, and then approaching appropriate people for assistance;
- when appropriate, being willing to ask questions;
- being committed to personal growth and development;
- being committed to the success of the firm;
- outlining and implementing a career path; and
- understanding and meeting firm expectations.

The mentee responsibilities mimic responsibilities of the mentor and might include:

- learning as much about the firm as possible through the orientation process, orientation and reference manual, and mentoring program;
- actively participating in the mentoring program;
- attending scheduled events and meetings as required;
- developing and implementing a personal business plan;
- being pro-active in developing professional relationships with others in the firm;
- actively seeking work if the assigned workload is not meeting goals;
- actively identifying and attending CLE programs to enhance legal skills as well as other professional development skills;
- understanding and exhibiting the core values of the firm;
- understanding and contributing to the firm vision;
- providing feedback regarding the firm mentoring program when requested; and
- participating in the lawyer evaluation program including performing a self-assessment, if requested.

Elements of a Strong Mentoring Program

Successful mentoring programs have several elements in common even when implemented in a variety of different firm cultures. Understanding firm culture is crucial to effective implementation of a mentoring program.

Goals and Objectives

For the program to be successful, goals and objectives should be identified, agreed upon, then used to drive the elements of the program. Goals define what the mentoring program will achieve, and the objectives outline how it will be done. Firm vision, mission, core values, and culture will lead the development of goals and objectives and should be created in accordance with the firm's strategic plan. Samples include:

Goals

- The mentee develops the skills and knowledge to become a successful and profitable lawyer.
- The mentee develops the skills and knowledge necessary to become a leader.

- The mentee develops an understanding of the firm culture.
- The mentee understands and follows firm policies and procedures.
- The mentee learns the firm client service philosophy.

Objectives

- The mentor/mentee will meet once a month to ensure effective communication.
- The mentor/mentee will agree to the mentee professional and personal goals.
- The mentor/mentee will define expectations of each other.
- The mentor/mentee will identify opportunities to provide mutual feedback.
- The mentor/mentee will identify time commitments needed by mentor/mentee.
- The mentor/mentee will identify the number of meetings specifically for evaluation discussions.
- The mentor/mentee will agree upon the confidentiality of the relationship, what it means and how it will be maintained.
- The mentor/mentee working dynamics will be outlined and agreed upon.

Organization and Structure

A successful mentoring program can be either formal or informal. There may be in-person and virtual components. It may be integrated into recruitment, orientation, or retention efforts. It may be a part of or responsible for the entirety of a new lawyer training program. Whichever organization and structure the firm chooses, mutual understanding of the mentor/mentee and consistent implementation are key. Two essential aspects also include assigning a responsible person(s) and defining the level of engagement expected.

Established Guidelines

Encapsulating the program in writing ensures all stakeholders involved understand the information and can reference it throughout the program. Written materials should include:

- the firm vision, mission, and core values;
- a description of the firm culture;
- the goals and objectives of the mentoring program;

- a timeline of regular communications;
- a sample agenda for the mentor/mentee meetings;
- the mentor's role and responsibilities;
- the mentee's role and responsibilities;
- a sample personal business plan;
- a description of the assessment and evaluation process; and
- a description of the reporting responsibilities and process.

The Pairing Process

When deciding who will be paired as mentor and mentee, the firm should consider various personal characteristics of the mentor and mentee like work habits, identities, personalities, and external interests. Also, the time the mentor has available to serve and the amount of time the mentee might require should be considered. Acceptable ratios of mentees to mentor will need to be established to ensure mentee loads are equitable. The practice areas of each, the needs of the mentee versus the qualities and skills of the mentor, and other factors affecting the relationship and the growth of the mentee may also be considerations in pairing.

Qualified Mentors

Strong mentors are a must. Without mentor buy-in, the program will not work. Some mentors have natural instincts and others will need to be developed. The development of qualified mentors can take time and should be an additional focus of a training and mentoring program. What is a strong mentor? The firms must collectively identify the characteristics of successful mentors and then create a plan to develop those characteristics in others.

Mentors must also be rewarded for their contribution to the growth and development of the new lawyers who successfully grow and develop within the mentoring program. All firm partners should participate in the development of younger lawyers. But for those partners that go above and beyond and serve as mentors, recognition through compensation or some other form is necessary and appropriate.

Effective Communication

An effective communication process is essential to the successful implementation of the mentoring program. At all levels within the firm—be it firm to mentor, firm to mentee, mentor to mentee, mentee to mentor, mentor to firm, or mentee to firm, information sharing, and knowledge distribution—must be performed consistently and with the appropriate level of transparency.

Firm lawyers, firm administration, and firm staff are involved in ensuring the mentoring program is successful. Each will play a role in assisting new lawyer development and growth. While the mentoring program outlines the process, the people will implement it.

Communications processes can include:

- announcing when a new lawyer joins the firm;
- indicating the mentor to be assigned to the new lawyer;
- creating a timeline for people to meet the new lawyer;
- creating a welcome schedule for the new lawyer;
- implementing the mentor/mentee program; or
- sharing success stories of the mentee.

The Evaluation Process

Sharing the success of the mentoring program will motivate people to remain involved and committed to the program. Narrating and reporting on this success requires reviewing the mentoring program annually to ensure it is meeting its established goals and objectives. Input for this review may be sought from mentors and mentees regarding the advantages, disadvantages, weaknesses, and strengths of the program to help determine what, if anything, can be improved. Additionally, committing to revising the program as firm culture changes, to increasing program efficiencies, and to incorporate cutting-edge mentoring strategies is an actionable way to continue to get involvement and commitment from the firm team.

Conclusion

Organized orientation and structured training directly and indirectly fuel profitability, client succession, client retention, client development, management succession and many other firm management business operations which depend on the success of individual lawyers and the entirety of the firm team. As previously mentioned, building, developing, and supporting the team of a law firm is much the same as guiding and growing a track team. Investing the time in training runners—or new lawyers—and utilizing experienced runners—or firm leaders—as mentors results in a firm team that will persist and achieve success.

Chapter 6
Establishing and Managing Effective Practice Groups

Chuck Roberts

Overview

Although this chapter is titled *Establishing and Managing Effective Practice Groups*, the term managing is used in the title only because it's a term commonly used within the legal industry. Superior performance is far easier to achieve when you focus on leadership, which is proactive, rather than management, which is reactive. This is because proactive leadership has a dramatic, positive impact on employee alignment and engagement which are key to enabling your firm to achieve more with fewer resources, improve morale in a way that results in greater client satisfaction and leads to more referrals, and sustain simultaneous growth of both revenue and profitability, even under challenging economic conditions. So, from this point forward, the focus of this chapter will be on how to lead the establishment and operation of effective practice groups.

Defining Your Purpose

To effectively lead and select appropriate practices for your firm, you must first be able to articulate why your firm exists—its Purpose. Once you know your firm's Purpose, the identification of appropriate practice areas for your firm and how to lead their operation become more obvious.

Many firms conduct strategic planning and during this process define their Mission, Vision, and Values, but fail to define their Purpose. Yet, Purpose is the basis on which all decisions should be evaluated. A firm's Mission defines *what* your firm does and for whom, but the Purpose defines *why* your firm exists. So, without knowing your firm's Purpose it's difficult to make sound decisions about establishing practices.

When employees of a firm are asked why the firm exists, it's not unusual for them to say it's to make money. However, in conversations I've had with people who have started up companies (and having started many of them myself), not one that I know of has started their firm for the express purpose of making money. The start-up is driven by some other passionate motive. While the Purpose of well-known firms is often not well documented, it's generally accepted that Disney's Purpose was to create happiness, and Steve Jobs's Purpose of founding Apple was to put a ding in the universe, which he certainly accomplished. With every decision, including what practices to establish, the question then becomes: "Does this action support our Purpose?"

So, the first step to establishing effective practices for your firm is understanding and articulating your Purpose. Then, when you choose practices that fulfill this Purpose, their growth and profitability are much more likely to be fueled by passion.

Matching Practice Choice with Demand

It's normal to feel concern about whether there is sufficient demand for the services involved in the practice you choose to launch, or to want to time the launch of a new practice with market trends, such as emerging issues surrounding Artificial Intelligence. However, these are not key drivers for the success of practice initiatives.

As long as you avoid obvious poor choices such as launching a practice targeted at air rights in a rural community where the tallest building is three stories, focusing on mining natural resources if you're located in a highly urbanized area, or pursuing issues pertaining to contracts with artists in the music industry when you're not in a recognized hub of musical activity such as Nashville or Los Angeles, you can succeed by capturing a substantial share of the existing market, which is accomplished by properly differentiating your firm from existing and potential competitors. In fact, in most circumstances it's possible to achieve sustainable growth of both revenue and profitability by proper differentiation even during periods of shrinking demand, simply by taking market share from competitors.

As for timing the launch of a practice to capitalize on a new trend, this is usually a costly and risky proposition. The competitive advantage you achieve by being early to market typically doesn't last long enough to recover your investment in achieving speed to market because competitors will be following close behind you. You are likely to achieve a superior return on investment by creating and adopting innovative operational practices that provide long-lasting benefits and are difficult for competitors to detect, and even more difficult for them to replicate.

Generalist or Specialist

In establishing practice areas for your firm, you must determine whether your Purpose is best fulfilled by being what many call a "full service" firm or having a well-defined field of specialty. The desire to capitalize on any opportunity that emerges encourages many firms, especially smaller firms, to take the path of generalization, thinking that they don't want to give up any potential revenue. But the majority of clients we've queried express the desire to engage a specialist, not a generalist, citing their perception that the representation they receive will be of a higher caliber and produce better results. Whether this outcome is true or not matters less than the fact that this is a common perception, and from the client's perspective, perception equals reality, and reality is what drives their selection process.

Can a firm be perceived as a specialist in more than one practice? Absolutely. However, you're more likely to be successful if you position your firm as having narrowly focused practices that provide related services, or that provide services within a single market segment or closely related market segments.

Teamwork and Cross-Functionality

One of the key challenges with establishing a new practice is incurring the costs of an initiative before enough clients and engagements are obtained to make the new practice self-sufficient. This challenge can be effectively addressed by encouraging teamwork and cross-training among your attorneys so they want to support each other and are capable of supporting one another. Using this approach, clients are the firm's clients rather than "belonging" to a practice or a lead attorney. Further, the firm is afforded greater flexibility with respect to staffing engagements and keeping attorneys and support personnel billable, and fewer attorneys are needed to generate the same or more revenue and profit. Individual differences in capabilities are recognized, valued, and leveraged for the firm's advantage. For example, attorneys who are highly proficient at bringing in work are given higher sales goals with a deliberate reduction in their billable time recognizing that their contribution to building a larger practice far outweighs the revenue they can generate by billing their time. Conversely, attorneys who are not proficient at bringing in work are given the goal of maintaining very high billable utilization with the understanding that their ineffectiveness at bringing in work will only drive up the firm's indirect overhead at the expense of lost revenue.

To facilitate effective teamwork, the metrics by which you recognize and reward performance need to encourage the desired behaviors. If you want a staff that can operate cross-functionally, then that attribute needs to be identified as having value in the appraisal and compensation process. If you want to discourage silo behavior, then bonuses need to be structured so that a large percentage of the reward is based on how the entire enterprise performs instead of solely on individual practice or individual personal achievements. Deliberate and well-crafted changes in metrics of this nature have created overnight increases in teamwork and driven firms to a higher level of performance within the constraints of their available resources.

The Approach to Launching a New Practice

A new practice can be launched one of four ways: cold start, warm start, lift-out, or acquisition. Each approach has its characteristic pros and cons, but experience has demonstrated that three factors have the greatest influence on which approach is best for your firm. These three factors are the time required to achieve a sustainably profitable operation, the desire to reduce risk exposure associated with making a major decision, and financial requirements. Understanding the interaction of these three parameters can help you make an informed decision regarding the approach to launching a new practice for your firm.

A cold start, which means launching a new practice with no existing contracts, is typically characterized as the slowest to achieve sustainable profitability and highest risk of failure, but it is generally a low cost approach. The high risk of failure is usually increased further if the initiative is led by a new hire. This is because while it's typical for some clients to follow an attorney, there are many factors that can interfere with this happening. And, despite rigorous reference checks and a proven track record of past performance, market conditions may be different today than when their prior track record was established and due to the time lag associated with business development you likely won't know if you made a good hiring decision until you're six to 18 months into the initiative. And, at that point, you've made a substantial investment and may be showing little or no progress.

A warm start means launching a new practice with a small number of existing contracts, often provided by an existing client who has engaged your firm for your other established areas of expertise. This is the next slowest to achieve sustainable profitability, and the second highest risk of failure, but it is the least cost because the revenue stream, although limited, helps to cover some or all of the cost of the start-up. The risk tends to be greater when the practice initiative is led by a new hire for the same reasons as cited for the cold start.

A lift-out involves hiring a partial or entire practice from a competing firm. This usually results in capturing clients from the competing firm, thereby significantly reducing the time to achieving sustainable profitability and significantly reducing the risk of failure. However, a lift-out typically involves significantly greater initial cost, careful negotiation and timing of coordinated employment offers, and attention to the existence of restrictive non-compete arrangements. Once the lift-out is executed, integration of the new employees can be challenging because they sometimes stick together rather than assimilating into your existing employee population, and depending on the number of employees involved, they can have a significant impact on your firm's culture. This can be a positive, energizing impact, or a negative and disruptive impact depending on how well you've vetted their compatibility with your existing firm, and the objectives you're trying to achieve.

Acquisitions vary widely in their impacts depending on whether you choose to acquire a struggling firm, or one that is characterized by growth and profitability that are similar to or greater than those of your firm. Unless you have directly applicable experience performing successful turnarounds, acquiring a struggling firm is not recommended. Acquiring a successful firm after rigorous due diligence is a great way to immediately add to both your revenue and profitability while adding one or more new practice areas. While this approach typically requires the greatest up-front investment, acquisition of a profitable firm can be self-funding. Acquisitions are typically characterized by moderate risk, but this exposure can be significantly reduced by careful attention to the deal structure and integration over the 12 months following the transaction.

Firm and Practice Scalability and Succession

Organizing a law firm by practice rather than geography or market segment provides the foundation for scalability. However, it is only the foundation. Scaling up a firm requires leaders, and those leaders can only come from two places: being developed in-house or hired from outside the firm. Neither approach should be used exclusively. Promoting from within encourages attorneys already in the firm to perform, but relying entirely on internal resources can limit the speed of growth and restrict the firm's exposure to ideas and practices from outside the firm or outside the industry that have the potential to dramatically improve performance. While tenure is valuable, it's also a weakness because it amplifies the effect of leaders not being aware of what they don't know.

Part of the firm's Integrated Strategic, Tactical, and Financial Plan should therefore include an initiative to identify and develop one or more successors for every position in every practice and fulfill this need with a deliberate mix of internal and external candidates.

If your firm is currently organized by geographic or market sector profit centers, it's wise to shift to a practice-oriented profit center structure sooner rather than later, as such reorganizations are easier to implement when the firm is small. When reorganization is needed, note that revolutionary change is characterized by a higher success rate and lower cost than evolutionary change, and that the change initiative should be led by an individual who possesses transformational leadership skills rather than only transactional leadership skills.

Many firms hesitate to reorganize because they fear losing historical performance data that was tracked using different profit centers. However, such data is generally not a significant factor in future performance, so reorganization provides an excellent opportunity to restructure your chart of accounts and the format of your financial reports in a way that groups fixed, variable, and discretionary expenses so that it's easier for leaders to analyze and focus on controllable factors. Although it's often used as the basis for establishing budgets, most firms would do well to reduce their reliance on historical practices and take a fresh approach to establishing a budget that reduces habitual spending and shifts to investing in actions likely to produce a superior return on investment. This includes analyzing the performance of your individual practice areas, and service lines within each practice area so you can focus your initiatives and investments where they will provide the greatest benefit.

Lawyer Needs

Alignment, engagement, and morale have a larger impact on firm performance than most leaders recognize, and these aspects of attorney behavior are strongly influenced by the attorney's relationship with their supervisor whether working in a direct line or matrix configuration. Supervising attorneys who believe that their subordinates must simply conform to their wishes are likely to experience disappointing results. Proactive leadership can dramatically reduce the amount of reactive management required to run a practice or a firm.

When designating one of your attorneys as the leader of a new or existing practice, you can help them by clearly articulating how success will be defined (and that typically has at least two components: how the client defines success and how success is defined by your firm), along with specific quantitative and qualitative goals, a schedule for achieving those goals, and a small array of Key Performance Indicators (KPIs) or metrics by which you will evaluate their performance. It's also very important to their success to confirm that ample financial and human resources are made available to them to facilitate success. This last item is particularly important for setting up a new practice. This last step is also key to preventing your firm from simultaneously launching more initiatives than can be properly staffed or funded.

In addition to those things, two of the most basic needs of all lawyers, and certainly those who you expect to start or lead a practice, are respect for their capabilities and accomplishments and feeling that they are supported when that support is needed most. And, there are three simple things that you can do to meet those needs of the attorneys you supervise.

The first action that proactively demonstrates respect for an attorney's capabilities and accomplishments is to provide appropriate levels of direction and support when making an assignment to a subordinate. The appropriate levels of direction and support depend on the individual's task-specific competence and commitment. The greater the competence, the less direction is appropriate. Over directing shows a lack of respect. But, when assigning a task that is unfamiliar to the attorney, direction is not only appropriate but desirable, or the attorney may perceive that you're setting them up for failure. When the assignment involves work the attorney enjoys or is eager to perform to learn a new skill, little support or encouragement is needed. However, if it involves a task they detest, support and encouragement are essential.

The second action that proactively demonstrates respect for an attorney's capabilities and accomplishments is to provide recognition. Note that recognition does not need to be monetary. The more public the recognition, and the more specific you can be about the attorney's contribution and achievements, the better. Specificity has tremendously greater positive impact than expressing general appreciation because it signals that you really care and were paying attention to details of the accomplishment. Providing recognition in front of the firm's executive leadership team is very powerful because it shows that you are helping the attorney in their quest for advancement.

The third action is to have a dialogue with the attorney about their personal and professional goals and then identify specific ways that you can help them to achieve their goals. This can involve mentoring them, supporting their involvement in training workshops to improve or develop new skills, or finding was to get them involved in matters that will help them develop a broader skill set in areas of the practice or in other practices in which they have an interest.

Making the proactive effort to meet the needs of attorneys you supervise generally increases their desire to work under your direction and lays the foundation for them to support you and the achievement of your goals.

Chapter 7
Leadership in Law Firms

Breana Jackson

Close your eyes. Imagine yourself behind a podium. You've been invited by a local university to give a commencement speech to its graduating class—the class of 2028. You are standing in front of a crowd filled with hopeful law students. What do you say? Who do you quote to motivate the future lawyers in the room? Do you speak similarly to clients? What ways of thinking do you return to during times of stress like this? Now, open your eyes. Abraham Lincoln? Nelson Mandela? Steve Jobs? Who came to mind?

Throughout history, we have not only labeled but named some of our most inspiring and prolific leaders as *great*—Alexander, Catherine, Cyrus, Ashoka. Why? What made their leadership the stuff of legend? How have they permeated the collective memory of the globe? A more modern hot take—leadership doesn't come from the man (or woman) on high, it is inherent in all individuals. To what degree? That is what firms need to work to identify in their partners and associates to leverage leadership for firm success.

Leadership: What It Is and What It's Not

Can't quite put your finger on it? Charisma? Power? Leadership? What is it about the partners in your firm that commands attention? A following. An allegiance. There are likely a variety of leaders and leadership styles in every firm. These styles and the effectiveness of your leaders may be debated along measures of difference. Firm culture, demographics, and even geographic area may contribute to the conversation about what type of leadership is needed for firm success. First, the firm needs to decide what leadership is and what leadership is not. What attributes should you consider when trying to develop your own individualized leadership skills as well as the skills of others within your law firm?

Given vs. Earned

Much like trust, leadership within the firm may be given or earned. Partners and other law firm leaders may *give* someone a powerful position within the firm through an appointment. This decision can be arbitrary or made after careful consideration. However, that leader is unlikely to be supported, develop a loyalty from firm members, or be effective if the collective group does not share the view that the new leader has *earned* the position. Firm members may demand to have witnessed the new leader grow in their experience, find their voice within the firm, and demonstrate their ability to lead the firm into the future.

Self-Appointed vs. Trust Building

How does a leader come to be? Some may call *self-appointed* leaders: natural leaders. These types of leaders are usually described as the loudest, most outspoken, and most commanding person in the room. Less commonly, natural leaders are described as the firm's rainmaker or the person who makes solving firm issues seem effortless. These leaders are often the most visible in a firm and may feel the need to take charge whether they have earned a leadership spot or not. Although stepping into action may make these individuals seem like obvious candidates for leadership positions, they may not actually be the most truly influential people in your firm. Consider those who have made a point of *building trust* before leading the way. They may be described as consistent, dependable, generous, or perceptive.

Constant vs. Consistent

Alexander the Great was *given* his throne through inheritance. He was deemed a *self-appointed* leader who decided to expand the Macedonian kingdom. According to the oracle, he was the son of Zeus-Ammon and was destined to *constant* rule over the Persian Empire until his death. For much of human history, this is how the story of world leaders has read—a power grab and the strategy of keeping it. It is imperative to recognize that despite this reoccurring narrative, successful leadership is not *constant*, but *consistent*. Partners with their name on the door may have been successfully leading the firm for years; however, their name doesn't always translate into a firm full of loyal associates—and post-succession, their influence may be lost. Their consistency is what lives on. Commitments to firms do not necessarily come from following its leaders, but investing in the mission, vision, and values instituted by those leaders. A law firm will not survive without positioned leaders that are willing to prioritize the firm. In the last five years, law firms have seen an unprecedented increase in turnover among associates. As young lawyers weave their way through firms, they look for something they want to invest in. Successes in retention correlates to whether incoming lawyers see *consistent* adherence to firm values by its leaders.

Individual vs. Team Oriented

One myth of leadership is that it exists in the *individual*—the person you think of quoting when drafting a commencement speech. History gives us a second option. It shows us that *teams* of complementary talent—like the 1980 USA hockey team who played the Miracle on Ice or the Selección de fútbol de Argentina who's blue and white stripes are as widely known as Messi himself—can provide leadership just as effectively. Successful leadership is built by reflecting on gaps in your own abilities, identifying those missing abilities in others, and inviting them to join your team. Acknowledging new lawyers' contributions to the firm and placing rising leaders in places where they feel empowered can help build a foundation of team leadership.

Leadership is:

Earned
Trust Building
Consistent
Team Oriented

Leadership is not:

Given
Self-Appointed
Constant
Individual

A Note on Leadership vs. Management

Both *leadership* and *management* have elusive definitions. They may differ when sourced from news pundits, professors, or firm management consultants. Difference can also be heard among those who are most widely or notoriously known for their charisma and power in action—think about the range of definitions you may get from Albus Dumbledore, Daenerys Targaryen, or Darth Vader. It is also semantics. The meaning we make of each word may vary between us. One way to reframe the construction of these definitions and, therefore, make them useful for your firm, is to delineate between where the motivation for either originates. Is it intrinsic or extrinsic?

Intrinsic motivation surfaces leadership while extrinsic motivation fits the needs of management. Intrinsic leadership fields inspiration from followers while management's extrinsic rewards rely on obedience of others. Followers grow into committed associates and partners while obedient employees meet expectations to progress in their careers. Leaders and managers are both key in engaging your firm in successful practice and are necessary to make the bottom line black.

Leadership Prospectives: What's Right for Your Firm?

Positional Leadership

Positional Leadership tends to be where the ideas of leadership and management are most conflated. There is a visual, structural component to positional leadership as it holds a title, an office with a window, or some other benefit not shared by everyone in the firm. It places an individual at a *position* of heightened power and/or authority. This type of leadership is common in law firms. The confusion comes from the place of power. Though someone may be positioned to wield power and decision making, it does not necessarily mean they are seen as a *leader.* Positional leadership really provides an opportunity for social influence and firm management simultaneously and in mutually beneficial ways. It is the vision and the implementation, the trust and the accountability. When these two work harmoniously, successful outcomes become cyclical and innate, contributing to a positive feedback loop. When creating positions of leadership and appointing human beings to fill them, firms should carefully consider how that new leader may balance the ideas of leadership and management before they are introduced to the role. Are they more intrinsically or extrinsically motivated? Does your firm culture value individual or team-oriented leaders?

Pace Leadership

"Show me the money!" As one of the most memorable lines from *Jerry McGuire* (1996), this phrase came to epitomize the value of rainmaking—or *pace*—leadership in the 1990s. Just like the athlete and sports agent in the film, many managing partners are motivated by their bottom line. Utilizing rainmakers as an element of your firm's success is smart; however, reliance on the loudest opinion or a singular focus on the money makers can sometimes leave the most toxic members of a firm with the most influence. It may also breed the wrong type of competitive spirit among colleagues. Rather than finding a way to utilize each lawyer's strength, pace leadership runs the risk of remaining laser focused on firm profits. In the long term it can start to pit functional areas of the firm against each other. Branding, administration, business development, people, client service/work, innovation, processes/efficiencies, historical—each key functional area will also begin to focus on the bottom line rather than the overall longevity of the firm.

When we reflect on what leadership is and what it is not, we find that both positional and pace leadership are not in fact *leadership* at all, rather they are components of *management* and are important to firm functionality. When addressing leadership for the firm success, however, we must look beyond hierarchy and performance to the value of mutual success. Pitting colleague against colleague in a race to profit quickly leaves the firm void of substance—and in times of crisis, these firms may dissolve. The antidote to runaway management issues may be rethinking leadership as relational.

Relational Leadership

Relational Leadership is about combining all the key areas of the team to fulfill a recipe for success. In the words of John Wooden, American basketball coach and player,

> *"I worry that business leaders are more interested in material gain than they are in having the patience to build up a strong organization, and a strong organization starts with caring for their people."*

As a coach, Wooden would have cared, would have been attuned to his players' strengths as well as any gaps in ability. This knowledge would have helped him recruit new players that showed skill in the areas where the team was lacking. Inviting those players to join him at the University of California, Los Angeles (UCLA) may be the very reason he took the Bruins on to win ten National Conference Athletic Association (NCAA) national championships. Giving each player the room to grow and the support they needed likely made all the difference. Likewise in a law firm, bucketing talent and empowering your team to perform to their highest level may require some investment in knowing who they are as people.

Relational Leadership not about the me, it's about the we. What does it look like? It is empowering partners, staff, and associates alike to lead and to follow uniquely from their key function in the firm.

Practical Implementation

Leadership concepts are useful, but how do you put them into practice? Let us explore relational leadership and how to capitalize on it for your firm's benefit.

Firm Processes

Ready for a change? Start with low stakes firm processes. Take a few days or week, pay particular attention to the flow of your office. Who do you see? What are they doing? Do you feel any pain points? Hear anything that catches your attention? Record your observations and then ask yourself—and your team—three simple questions:

1. Where are things going well?
2. Does anything need our immediate attention?
3. How do we take one step closer to realizing our vision?

Once the temperature of current firm process has been taken, put leadership into action. Survey the entirety of the firm. Mass participation is key, so keep the survey short, letting contributors know the number of questions and time they should allot to complete. Questions should be qualitative and holistic in nature, asking for answers specific to each firm member. Questions may be:

- What is the biggest challenge in your role currently?
- What talents/skills do you want to work on developing?

- What functional aspects, processes, or values of our firm at large need to be revisited?
- How can the firm help you succeed?
- How can the firm help support your life balance?

Be sure to set aside a significant amount of time to process answers and look for themes. Also, be sure to share the results of your findings with those who made the investment of their time, talent, and ideas to further improve your firm.

Bucketing Your Talent

To support change management, align your talent. Hiring to lead starts with identifying the traits necessary to round out the talent in your firm.

Trait vs. Talent

Trait: A differentiating personality factor. Examples include hard-working, reliable, detail-oriented, social, resilient, optimistic.

Talent: A natural ability and interest in a specific area. Examples can be understanding how to use technology, staying up to date on current trends, connecting with a particular group—clients, staff, associates, creating community.

Step One: Identify current firm traits and talents
Who do people in your firm go to for advice or help with:

- Client issues?
- Technology needs?
- A second pair of eyes?
- Solving colleague disagreements?

It may be helpful to have senior members of the firm individually walk through the strategic plan and identify who in their firm tends to lead in each area. Likewise, it may also help to have senior members identify the most valuable talents of each person, what they rely on them for, and any kind of expertise they may have. Chart out the buckets of talent that correspond to the needs of your strategic plan—people/human capital, technology, financial, and so on.

Step Two: Identify areas where the firm needs more
Who fills the technology bucket? No one? Well, we've identified a talent your firm is looking to acquire via a future hire. Create a collective list of traits and talents the firm is looking to use to fill its empty or shallow

buckets—grit, team-oriented, proactive, tech savvy, substantively well-versed, able to build relationships across difference. Now, you are aware of what you have and what you are looking to recruit.

Job Title: Talent (bucket) needed.
Job Description: Combinations of traits and talent necessary to fill talent bucket.

Step Three: Filter candidates through holistic metrics

The hiring process can be complex and daunting. Let's break it down and consider some brief guidelines particular to finding future leaders among your candidates.

The resume will give an overview of what experience has contributed to the candidate's talent development and what they can bring to the firm. Don't forget, even though a resume may display only 70% of the *talent* you're trying to recruit, read on for indications the applicant has *traits* worth adding to the firm. For instance, younger lawyers may not have well-established buckets of talent, but if they display a willingness to learn, they may be a much better addition to the team than an extensively talented, stubborn candidate. Bringing them into interview is a holistic way to explore who is beyond the resume.

During an interview, candidates will share their experience and discuss their talents. Be intentional in crafting and asking questions that draw out their traits as well. If the firms' brand is being innovative, forward thinking, and cutting edge, then interview questions should provide the candidate with a platform to display their traits. Examples:

- Tell me about software you've used to help your practice. How did that software help you serve your clients?
- Walk me through a tech trend our firm should adopt to compete in the marketplace?
- How do you create efficiencies within your practice or position?

These questions prompt the candidate to speak to their technological knowledge, comfortability, mindset, and foresight—or lack thereof. If the traits displayed by the candidate may fill some existing gaps on your team or build upon existing strengths, then you may have a successful candidate to hire.

Step Four: Onboard with talent development direction

New hires are made for a variety of reasons. In their first months at the firm, be intentional about acknowledging what new lawyers bring to the team, what benefits the firm, and give opportunities for the new hires to employ their traits and practice their talents. Over this time, leaders in the firm can start to identify the valuable traits and talents of the new hires and encourage them to get involved where they are most needed.

Relational leadership pairs well with *successional leadership*. With relational leadership, the leader prioritizes the 'we' and is comfortable transitioning their leadership to facilitate long-term firm success. Firms are at an early advantage for long-term success when they onboard new hires and encourage them to consider working toward a future decision-making role within the firm. Leadership is developed over time. If you wait to develop leadership in members of your firm until you are ready to put them into a leadership position, you are too late. By that time, it is likely that young lawyers have already grown into leaders but their leadership was built underground and may not be committed to serving the same overall, consistent goals as the firm.

Conclusion

Leadership may reside within anyone in the firm. Management is the function of a few. Decision-makers and mentors can identify the traits and talents of those they work with and empower them to be relational leaders in their own sphere of influence. The firm will benefit from the collective ownership felt from retention, to innovation, through succession and beyond—but only if its leaders are committed to and consistent with firm values. So, back to the commencement speech—which leader will you quote?

> *"It is with passion, courage of conviction, and strong sense of self that we take our next steps into the world."*
>
> —Elle Woods the Great?

Chapter 8
Risk Management and the Role of Law Firm General Counsel

Ronald Richman and Michael Beaver

Introduction

In ancient days (in law-firm speak, as recently as the 1970s), law firms ran themselves as insular, professional societies. Day-to-day decisions about client intake, ethical compliance, and client complaints were left to the individual discretion of the partners. Legal malpractice claims were rare. The firm's own legal needs were a relatively occasional minor distraction.

Two major factors have drastically changed the landscape. One is the explosive growth of legal malpractice claims over the last 50 years, including a proliferation of state bar complaints, which now involve not only alleged simple mistakes (e.g., missing a deadline) but also a host of situations including business or commercial transactions which crater before or after closing; strategy and staffing; unexpected or unanticipated adverse judgments; and just about anything that the firm (or one of its professionals) either might have done better or a risky strategy or tactic that the firm or one of its professionals should not have taken. As a consequence, legal malpractice insurance has become exponentially more important (as well as expensive), and insurers have become active participants in law firm risk management. In addition, large institutional clients are requiring law firms to carry a certain level and type(s) of insurance as a condition to receiving referrals. A second factor has been the growth of law firms from small groups of lawyers with homogeneous practices to larger organizations involving multiple specialized practices, and multi-jurisdictional (even international) areas of service. This in turn has caused the average law firm to become a sophisticated business, operating in a highly regulated environment and with internal legal needs not unlike those of a similarly-sized corporation. A third factor is the ever-increasing "bet the company" litigations, for example, pharmaceutical, product liability, IP, or emerging AI, where there exists the potential for a seven- or eight-figure adverse judgment.

Risk management, regulatory compliance and oversight of the firm's general legal needs are now vital to the success of law firms of virtually any size. Some firms, like some clients, still consider legal their own legal matters to be annoying business distractions. But many of the most successful firms have come to see risk and legal management as a strategic imperative. Increasingly these firms are devoting more time and resources to the general counsel position.

Corporations long ago reacted to the same concerns by hiring general counsel—lawyers employed on a part- or full-time basis to help bring legal input into the company's general strategy and decision making, as well as oversight of the company's legal needs. Law firms, while coming a little later to this party, now frequently designate general counsel for the same reasons the firms' clients did years ago. General Counsel, including in-house general counsel, also afford the law firm with a potential "cloak" of privileged and confidential attorney-client communications.

What Is Law Firm Risk Management

IBM defines "risk management" to mean "the process of identifying, assessing and controlling financial, legal, strategic and security risks" to an organization.[1] For a law firm, some of these potential risk factors are basically the same as faced by any business—for example, risk posed by employment claims, on-premises injury, cyber/security breaches, property damage/business interruption, and directors' and officers' liability (i.e., law firms that utilize a board of directors or similar management team). Some law firm risk is similar to general business risk but ***heightened*** by ethical duties imposed upon the legal profession—for instance, the risk of financial dishonesty (especially with regard to client trust funds), or cybersecurity (in

[1] www.ibm.com/think/topics/risk-management.

view of the profession's client confidentiality obligations and Health Insurance Portability and Accountability Act of 1996 ("HIPAA") regulations for law firms handling cases that may involve retention of medical records).

But a host of risks (and related activities) are unique to the practice of law and the business of law firms:

Risks Associated with Legal Malpractice

The risks associated with legal malpractice sometimes overlap with ethical non-compliance. Malpractice insurance is of course a central strategy for mitigating these risks. But that doesn't end the inquiry. Malpractice insurance needs and preferences must be carefully analyzed. What forms of coverage are to be included, with what policy limits? What risk retention/deductible levels are desired or required? Beyond core malpractice insurance, what types of related coverage may be needed, such as cybersecurity and financial dishonesty coverage? Resolving these questions is just the beginning of a risk mitigation strategy; it must also entail counseling and training firm lawyers on both identifying and assessing risk management issues, procuring and administering the coverage (including claim reporting renewal requirements), and working with the insurer, firm management, and firm personnel to create an ongoing culture and awareness of risk management, including identifying potential risk management claims and reporting such claims, or the potential for such claims, to the designated general counsel for the firm.

Risks Associated with the Intake of New Files

The firm must have specific and uniform guidelines on client intake procedures for opening new files with existing clients and also when deciding whether or not to take on a new or different client or new or different type of case. The first critical step in avoiding ethical conflicts, especially in mid-size or large firms, and those law firms with multi-jurisdictional practices, is to have a protocol for opening up a new file which law firms often refer to as the "business intake process." No file should be opened, whether it be from an existing client or a new client, without a defined "business intake process." The business intake process should include, at a minimum: identification of the attorney opening the file; if the file is coming from an existing client, the file number/prefix identification for this client; the name of the client (and this is a critical step, to be sure to identify the correct, full, legal name of the client); the parties involved, whether this be a litigation file, transactional file, general advice; the role of each party, i.e., are they adverse, co-party, non-opposing party); the description of the new business or legal work; whether an engagement letter has been prepared (essential for any new client);[2] whether an advanced fee or retainer has been obtained; and billing information, i.e., to whom the bills are to be sent.

It is recommended that the law firm utilize standard business intake forms, so that the same information is being provided for every file opening process. There are a number of services that offer template business intake forms. This business intake form, once completed, should go to the firm's designated client intake department. The client intake department should be well trained on reviewing and conducting conflict of interest searches and then reporting back to the attorney attempting to open the file if any "hits" come up on potential conflicts. Any "hits" on potential conflicts should go not only to the attorney attempting to open a new file, but to all other attorneys who have matters that are identified in any "hits" that come up on potential conflicts. The client intake department should then have a dialogue with all attorneys who are associated with any "hits"/ potential conflicts to determine if in fact any conflict exists. If there is a concern as to whether a potential conflict has arisen, this matter should then be referred to the firm's general counsel for review as to whether there is a potential conflict and if so, whether the potential conflict is or is not a waivable conflict. If the general counsel determines the conflict is not a waivable conflict, the new file should not be opened and the business intake process is concluded. If the general counsel determines there is waivable conflict, the final decision nevertheless rests with the client. A *written communication* should be sent to the client, outlining the potential conflict, why counsel believes this is a waivable conflict, and asking the client to acknowledge, in writing, that the client either waives the conflict or does not waive the conflict. If the client does not waive the conflict, then the file should not be opened and the business intake process is concluded.

---

[2] ABA Model Rules of Professional Conduct do not require a written engagement letter unless the engagement is based on a contingency fee. See ABA Model Rules of Professional Conduct 1.5 (c). However, some state jurisdictions require a written engagement letter for new clients. For example, CA Bus. & Prof. Code § 6148 requires a written engagement letter for any matter where fees are expected to exceed $1,000. In Oregon, ORS 20.340 also requires a written engagement letter for civil actions arising out of bodily injury, death or property damage, for contingency fee cases. In New York, attorneys are required to have a written engagement letter for all undertakings. See Part 1215 to Title 22 of the Official Compilation of Codes, Rules and Regulations of the State of New York.

A separate and distinct discussion should take place when an attorney attempts to open a new file for an area of law that is generally not undertaken by the lawyer or the firm, as a whole. Most law firms are moving away from the "one size fits all" mentality, meaning that the law firm will pretty much accept whatever "comes in the door." With more and more pressure on attorneys to generate new business and meet stringent billable goal requirements comes the urge for lawyers to take on matters where the attorney lacks the requisite experience or an area of law that the firm, as a whole, does not include in its core practice. While this may be more difficult to spot, as a part of the business intake procedure, if the business intake department identifies, from the business intake form provided, an area of practice that appears to be beyond the core practice of the law firm, the business intake department should notify the general counsel. The general counsel, in turn, can review the potential new file with the attorney attempting to open the new file and then present this to the firm's management committee for review and approval (or disapproval, wherein the file opening process will be terminated). It goes beyond mentioning that attempting to navigate around an area of law, or practice, that the lawyer and/or law firm is not well versed in, creates a substantial risk management problem and potential malpractice claim.

Risks Associated with the Termination of Client Work, Whether It Be Completion of the File or Withdrawal of Counsel

Termination of client work—which can be the result of completion of the engagement but may also result from lawyer departures, client firing, failure of the client to pay bills, or discovery of information that makes continued client representation ethically or practically unwise—is also freighted with both ethical compliance and risk management issues.

When the attorney believes client work for a particular file is completed, the attorney should send the client a *written confirmation* of the scope of the assignment, completion of the assignment (if the attorney deems necessary), a summary of the work performed and results, and notice that the attorney is closing the file.

Withdrawal from an active file, especially with an active litigation file, can be a minefield. Focusing on terminating the relationship with a difficult, potentially obstructive client and withdrawing from an active file, ABA Model Rule 1.16: Declining or Terminating Representation, paragraph (b)[3], provides certain guidelines. A lawyer may withdraw from representing a client if: "(1) withdrawal can be accomplished without material adverse effect on the interests of the client; (2) the client persists in a course of action involving the lawyer's services that the lawyer reasonably believes is criminal or fraudulent; (3) the client has used the lawyer's services to perpetrate a crime or fraud; (4) the client insists on taking action the lawyer considers repugnant or with which the lawyer has a fundamental disagreement; (5) the client fails to substantially fulfill an obligation to the lawyer regarding the lawyer's services and has been given reasonable warning that the lawyer will withdraw unless the obligation is fulfilled; (6) the representation will result in an unreasonable financial burden on the lawyer or has been rendered unreasonably difficult by the client; or (7) other good cause for withdrawal exits". Section 1.16(c) requires proper notice to or permission of a tribunal when terminating representation.

It is recommended that prior to terminating the representation of a client, the attorney should send the client *written notice* outlining, in detail, the perceived transgression(s), providing a means and method to cure the transgression(s), and a clear warning that if the client fails to cure the transgression, the attorney will withdraw. Focusing on active litigation files, for those attorneys accepting assignments from insurers, as panel counsel, terminating a client poses a more difficult problem. A "tripartite relationship" arises when an insurer hires a defense counsel to represent its insured. The defense counsel owes a duty to both the insurer and the insured. In certain jurisdictions, the insured (policyholder) and insurer are considered dual clients. In other jurisdictions, the primary obligation of the defense counsel is to the insured; a secondary obligation of the defense counsel is to the insurer. The tripartite relationship can pose ethical dilemmas for an attorney seeking to withdraw, especially when the insured fails to cooperate with the defense counsel. Many policies contain a duty to cooperate clause and if the insured fails to cooperate with the defense counsel, the insurer may deny or "pull coverage." The ethical dilemma for the defense counsel is how much information the defense counsel can and should disclose to the insurer regarding the conduct of the insured when the defense counsel seeks to withdraw from an active litigation.

---

[3] https://www.americanbar.org/groups/professional_responsibility/publications/model_rules_of_professional_conduct/rule_1_16_declining_or_terminating_representation/?login

In terms of seeking permission from a tribunal to withdraw, another ethical dilemma arises as to how much detail to provide to the court and, necessarily, opposing counsel in a motion to withdraw as such motion is a public document. ABA Model Rule 1.6: Confidentiality of Information provides stringent guidelines for protection of attorney-client confidentiality. Seeking advice from an outside ethics counsel, even if a law firm has its own in-house general counsel, is recommended.

Risks Associated with a Lawyer Leaving the Firm and Taking the Client(s) with Her or Him to a New Firm

Each jurisdiction may have its own prescribed rules and regulations regarding the situation where an attorney leaves the firm and intends to take certain clients with her or him. ABA Formal Op. 99–414 (1999) requires clients to be notified when an attorney departs a law firm and the departing attorney is responsible for the client's representation or played a significant role in the client's representation. A written notice should go to the client(s) advising of the attorney's departure and advising the client(s) that the client has the right to maintain the file with the current law firm and that the current law firm has the requisite skill and attorneys to continue the representation, or ask that the file be transferred to the departing attorney and his or her law firm. This is the ABA Formal Op. 19–489, Obligations Related to Notice When Lawyers Change Firms,[4] issued on December 4, 2019, confirming that it is the client's choice as to whether to stay with a current law firm or request that the file be transferred to the departing attorney and his or her new law firm. It is recommended that a written notice be sent to the departing attorney's clients, or client contacts, advising of the imminent departure of the attorney, advising whether the current law firm has the requisite skill and staff to continue the representation, or whether the client desires that the file be transferred to the departing attorney. If the client confirms, in writing, that the client wishes the file to be transferred to the departing attorney, the current law firm must honor that choice, make a timely transfer of the file documents and assist with any notices of withdrawal of counsel (in litigations, especially), and also ensure that no deadlines are missed during the transition. Once the transition is completed, the original law firm should advise the

[4] chrome-extension://efaidnbmnnnibpcajpcglclefindmkaj/https://www.americanbar.org/content/dam/aba/administrative/news/2019/12/aba_formal_opinion_489.pdf

client, in writing, that the file has been transferred and as of a certain date, the original firm has concluded its representation of the client and is closing their file. This creates a "clear line of demarcation" where the prior firm no longer has file responsibility, is no longer responsible for any future defects or mishaps, and the risk is transferred to the new attorney/new law firm.

Risks Associated with Lateral Hires

Each firm should have a protocol for the vetting of potential lateral hires. One obvious protocol is performing a comprehensive conflict check of cases and clients the potential lateral hire may bring over to the new law firm, and this should be performed by a firm's client intake department. Even if the potential lateral hire is not bringing cases or clients to the new firm, a comprehensive conflict check still needs to be performed so that a conflict does not arrive if and when the lateral hire begins work with the new law firm. The law firm seeking to hire a lateral should have a standard NDA (non-disclosure agreement) providing that the hiring law firm will keep all information about cases and clients identified by the lateral hire confidential and privileged. This NDA should put the potential lateral hire more at ease knowing that the information being provided will not be used by the hiring law firm in any inappropriate manner (such as to solicit such recently identified clients).

Risks Associated with Large Client Receivables

General counsel can get involved in attempting to collect/negotiate large receivables due and owing from current and/or former clients. Sometimes negotiations are just a matter of attempting to work out a payment plan. A more difficult scenario is when a client, present or former, ties its failure or refusal to pay an outstanding receivable on the ground the law firm's work was faulty, negligent, that is, tying its failure to pay on an allegation of malpractice. The general counsel will attempt to negotiate a payment and resolve any dispute regarding services performed by the law firm. Another problem arises when the client terminates its relationship with the law firm, fails or refuses to pay for outstanding legal services, and nevertheless demands the return of the file from the law firm. ABA Model Rule 1.16, Declining or Terminating Representation, paragraph (d), states that upon termination of representation, among other things, surrendering papers and property to the client. A caveat under 1.16(d) is: "The lawyer may retain papers relating to the client to the extent permitted by other law." Some jurisdictions (limited) allow for the attorney to retain the client file until the client has satisfied an outstanding account. The better practice seems to be that the attorney should return client files in order to stay clear of any possible state bar disciplinary action.

Day-to-day consultations with firm lawyers on ethical and risk management issues is a critical risk mitigation activity. The work of lawyers is complex. Unsurprisingly, this work generates frequent ethical and judgment issues which must be identified and resolved as early as possible. Often even a mistake which has already occurred can be fully resolved, with no loss, by this process. A firm must constantly educate its professionals on potential ethical and malpractice issues, and must constantly reinforce the necessity of early, easily-available consultation. A firm must have a risk management protocol and, as part of educating its professionals, identify to whom a potential risk management issue should be raised, whether it be in-house general counsel or outside general counsel, and how critical it is to advise the general counsel as soon as there exists the potential for a claim. In addition, each jurisdiction may have its own reporting requirements to the state bar regarding any discipline/sanctions handed down by a judge during the course of a litigation.

The Role of General Counsel

Simply put, someone in a law firm must be responsible for addressing the firm's risk management and other legal needs. There are multiple options—placing these concerns on the firm's managing partner, designating a part-time in-house general counsel, utilizing a full-time in-house general counsel, hiring an "outside" general counsel, or having a combination of an in-house counsel and a designated outside general counsel (or counsels) (all discussed next). Whatever option is chosen, a firm of any size should give serious consideration to the legal needs of the firm and how those needs are addressed.

Any law firm, like a business of similar size, has ongoing or sporadic need for all kinds of legal help, including, but not limited to: employment and HR issues, leasing and real estate, Intellectual Property ("IP") matters, vendor contracts, banking and transactional issues, and procuring and then renewing its insurance policies. This list could go on but this is fairly typical. A firm may have internal resources for dealing with these needs (although that is not always desirable).

Law firms have additional, industry-specific legal needs, however, including:

- Procuring and administering malpractice insurance (which often involves a degree of active partnership with the insurer), as well as other lines of business insurance. The general counsel needs to be aware of the claims history of the law firm, reporting requirements for any claim or potential claim, and needs to monitor the handling of claims by an outside panel counsel appointed to assist in claim handling and defense. The general counsel should be well versed in the types of coverage needed by a law firm including the basics: Professional Liability; EPL/ML [combined employment practices liability/management liability]; Property & Casualty [which includes property and general liability, earthquake, business auto, workers' compensation, umbrella, crime, fiduciary, special crime [kidnap for ransom] and workplace violence; and Cyber Liability. The general counsel should discuss with its broker the level of coverage, premiums, deductible, pier bench marking (coverage levels of similarly situated firms) and reporting requirements for a claim or potential claim.
- Handling day-to-day risk management issues (including ethics, conflicts, and risk management counseling within the firm).
- Managing the consideration and intake of new business.
- Advising on and administering the firm's own ownership structure—partnership/shareholder agreements, etc.
- Dealing with client requirements that have legal implications—for instance, outside counsel guidelines, staffing, or specialized conflicts demands.
- Advice and administration concerning the many ethics-related aspects of legal practice—e.g., business intake, fee agreements, co-counsel and referral agreements, lateral hiring and departure, law firm mergers, attorney marketing, and conflict waiver agreements.

How do law firms handle these needs? There are several common options:

- **The firm's managing partner** ("MP") may be tasked with handling risk management for the firm. The MP sometimes makes decisions alone, sometimes involves partners with some degree of expertise in the kinds of matters at hand, and also may be required to report to the firm's management committee (or Board of Directors) as to any risk management issue and recommended course of action. The MP also may recommend hiring outside counsel to help analyze and deal with internal risk management and legal issues or complex matters outside of the MP's area(s) of expertise. This approach may be cost-effective for very small firms, but it involves some significant attorney-client privilege risks, and the line between business judgment and independent legal judgment may be difficult to maintain for even the wisest, most seasoned law firm managers. It can be difficult for a law firm general manager to acquire and apply the specialized expertise that law firm risk management requires. Further, it is often too common for an MP to be mired down in other administrative, financial, or organizational tasks that require a significant amount of his or her time, thereby effectively diluting the risk management portion of the MP's duties.

- A firm may choose to retain **outside general counsel**. There are firms who specialize in providing general counsel services to small to mid-size firms. These firms often have extensive experience in risk management, human resources/employment, retirement and other benefit packages, real estate leases or acquisitions, and general law firm legal needs. They often are equipped to provide ethics and risk management counseling to individual firm lawyers. Some firms are even capable of integrating some of their own work product (for instance, a business intake protocol) into client operations.
- A law firm can designate a **part-time general counsel within the firm** to serve in a role analogous to the General Counsel role in a corporate environment. Even where the firm expects the time involvement to be relatively small (think 10–30 hours per month), there are significant advantages to having a designated internal lawyer. First of all, the internal lawyer will be most familiar with the firm, its lawyers, scope of practice, business policies and practices of the firm, staff members, organization of the law firm (i.e., departments, law practice groups, compensation), and, hopefully, all the pertinent risk management policies. In addition, that individual can become deeply familiar with insurance and other legal matters, and the designated role may be helpful in preserving internal attorney-client privilege (when the designated person is fully versed in applicable privilege principles).

- **Full-time in-house general counsel** is the ultimate step in bringing a law firm's legal needs in line with the firm's general strategic objectives. Of course, a full-time general counsel role makes sense mainly for fairly large firms (with at least 200 lawyers, for example), or unusual revenue-per-lawyer scenarios (think successful, larger contingent fee practices, for example). Full-time counsel is the best positioned to serve in the role with which corporations have grown familiar—a combination of well-informed strategic advice concerning a law firm's most sensitive needs, combined with the ability to oversee all day-to-day legal work for the firm. Even a full-time in-house general counsel should be ready to refer a matter to an outside special counsel in specialty areas of practice not within the wheelhouse of the in-house general counsel. This also applies to independent advice on claims and litigation against the firm.

In-House General Counsel vs. Outsourcing

It can be tempting to view these options in terms of cost. While cost is certainly a factor, it must be weighed against what is at stake. Internal legal issues can divide or even torpedo a law firm, be they related to risk management or ownership and general business concerns. Just as is true for corporate clients, selecting an approach to managing law firm risk and internal legal needs is a strategic choice.

Designating in-house general counsel, either on a part-time or full-time basis, has increasingly been the option selected by firms whose size can support it. There are no reliable metrics that suggest a size threshold, probably because the use of in-house general counsel can be so influenced by a firm's unique needs. For instance, a small firm practicing in a highly specialized, fast-developing field may be more inclined to designate in-house general counsel than a similarly sized "commodity practice" firm.

An old legal maxim holds that a lawyer who represents himself has a fool for a client. While perhaps true as applied to a lawyer's personal legal issues, the maxim doesn't necessarily hold for general counsel, who don't typically provide front-line representation of firm members in negotiation or ligation. That said, in-house general counsel (and firm management) must cautiously, consciously guard counsel's independent judgment.

Another reason that firms opt to designate general counsel within their ranks is the belief that this makes risk management and other legal input easier and quicker to access among firm lawyers. Outside general counsel firms are likely to differ, but many law firms believe that in-house counsel can make internal services available with fewer layers between attorney and client. And, as mentioned above, designating a full-time in-house general counsel should not restrict the in-house general counsel from seeking advice and potential representation from outside general counsel as the need arises. Often a combination of in-house and outside counsel works well for a firm. The in-house counsel provides immediate access for its lawyers. The in-house counsel should be knowledgeable and adept at handling day-to-day conflict issues, client intake issues, advice on avoiding or handling a potential claim should one arise, assisting with HR issues that do not arise to the level of a claim/complaint against the law firm. The outside counsel is usually a specialist, often a labor and employment attorney, corporate, or transactional counsel that can provide specialized services.

Compensation for In-House General Counsel

Whether a full- or part-time in-house general counsel, the law firm must come up with a compensation mechanism for the in-house general counsel so that it provides and prioritizes their role as in-house general counsel. If the in-house general counsel is full time, the law firm will have to pay them a reasonable and competitive salary. With part-time general counsel, law firms often opt to provide a base *additional* compensation for general counsel work, a separate "billing code," in addition to the in-house counsel's regular compensation, along with a corresponding reduction to the general counsel's minimum billable goal for the year. Usually the hours designated for in-house general counsel are "credited" toward the general counsel's annual billable goal requirement. The additional compensation provided to the general counsel should offset potential loss of income to the general counsel whose compensation, among other factors, is tied to his or her origination (dollars originated) and dollars worked.

Regardless of whether a law firm opts to have a full-time or part-time general counsel, it is critical that both the general counsel avail himself or herself of additional Continuing Legal Education ("CLE") training on risk management issues so that the in-house general counsel is trained and remains well-versed on the bevy of risk management issues a law firm faces as a part of its everyday practice and business model.

Chapter 9
Financial Management

Richard J. Wittbrodt

Introduction

Good law firm financial management governance is synonymous with good leadership, stewardship, and financial management. Effective governance within a law firm requires leaders who excel in financial management. Competent financial managers can ensure the firm's financial stability, which, in turn, fosters confidence and trust among partners, associate attorneys, and staff. This confidence in the firm's success enables partners and employees to wholeheartedly pursue the firm's goals. The overarching objectives of all law firms are identical: to deliver the finest advice and services to clients while increasing revenue. Proficient financial management directly contributes to enhanced profitability and productivity within the firm.

Sound financial management extends beyond the assessment of attorney productivity and profitability. It necessitates a focus on financial aspects such as budgeting, accountability, benchmarks, billing, and collections. A well-managed financial system empowers attorneys to dedicate their time to client matters, while allowing rainmakers to concentrate on marketing efforts to attract new clients. Good financial management also entails supporting associate attorneys aiming to build their careers within the firm and reap the benefits of eventual partnership. It calls for modernization, investments, succession planning, and strategies to ensure the firm's long-term sustainability.

Many businesses fail due to poor financial management. According to Lending Tree, "20.8% of private sector businesses in the U.S. fail within the first year. After five years, 48.4% falter, and after 10 years, 65.1% of businesses have failed."[5] Law firms are unique entities, as their ownership structure distinguishes them from most large American businesses, which are typically investor-owned.[6]

Statistics derived from studies of law firm failures reveal that one-third to one-half of law firm merger failures result from conflicts between partners, management, cultures, and personnel. Leadership is the root cause of these failures. Gross revenue alone is not a reliable indicator of failure; instead, mismanagement, over-extension, and over-expansion are the most common causes of such failures. Leadership often fails to prepare for unforeseen consequences, and it is this leadership failure that consistently emerges as the primary factor contributing to law firm failures. No level of management success can compensate for a breakdown in leadership.[7] Firms with highly skilled lawyers can falter due to inadequate business management. As Frank Wu, Chancellor of Queens College NY, wrote for the Huffington Post in 2015: "(V)ery few, if any, of the law firms that have 'failed' did so because the people employed there were subpar lawyers."[8] The goal of this chapter is to provide sound law firm financial management governance that you can use to be one of the successfully run law firms.

Productivity and Profitability

Starts with Hiring the Right People

Building a team of exceptional professionals begins with selecting the right individuals for your firm. It involves identifying candidates who possess genuine interest in the practice of law, particularly in your specific area of expertise. Look for individuals who treat others as equals, display curiosity, exhibit politeness, engage well in conversations, collaborate effectively in teams, demonstrate insightfulness and thoughtfulness, and are inherently motivated.

---

[5] Lending Tree, Devin Delfino, May 2023.

[6] John Morley, "Why Law Firms Collapse," Morley argues that the collapse of firms, their failure to reorganize, and their survival depend heavily on partner-owned and operated organizations, which often become entangled in a spiral of partner departures. Poor economic conditions, including decreased demand for services and mounting debt, pale in comparison to the significance of good governance and social factors in determining firm success.

[7] James Wittmack on LinkedIn, January 15, 2023.

[8] https://www.huffpost.com/entry/why-law-firms-fail_b_6827410?utm_campaign=share_email&ncid=other_email_o63gt2jcad4

To guide the hiring process effectively, it's crucial to align your firm's goals with the qualities you seek in candidates. While most law firms share the overarching objectives of delivering top-notch legal services and increasing profitability, it's also vital to consider the firm's culture in the selection process. Beyond the influence of the area of legal practice on culture, evaluate whether your firm embodies values such as honesty, teamwork, integrity, accountability, an appreciation for diversity, and recognition of the importance of life outside of work.

It's essential to recognize that no firm can cater to all preferences. Embrace what your firm uniquely offers, clearly define its culture, and reinforce it by making the right hires. The factors that contribute to a firm's culture stem from its behavioral norms and expectations. Articulate a set of core values for your firm and ensure clarity regarding behavioral and performance expectations, as well as the criteria for evaluating performance. Discuss aspects of social interaction within the firm and the style of firm management, including matters such as office attire, expectations around billable hours, office attendance, social gatherings, and even political affiliations, or lack thereof, as all these elements help define the firm's culture.

It's important to note that firm culture applies to both professional and nonprofessional staff, impacting everything from office dynamics to work environment. Questions like whether everyone's office doors are open or closed, whether it's a collaborative team-oriented setting or a collection of individual fiefdoms, underscore the significance of firm culture in the experience of all employees within the organization.

> In a 2022 Law Firm Culture Survey conducted by Major, Lindsey & Africa and "Law360 Pulse," over 750 respondents indicated the traits they would like to see more prominently reflected or valued in their law firms' cultures. The most commonly desired trait was an emphasis on training and mentoring (44%), followed by diversity (38%), support for attorney well-being and work-life balance (36%), succession/transition planning (36%), increased representation of women and people of color in leadership positions (33%), transparency (29%), and receptiveness to input (29%).[9]

---

[9] **Source (Reference a):** Reuters, Article by Roger E. Barton, November 17, 2022 https://www.reuters.com/legal/legalindustry/how-law-firms-can-embrace-new-emphasis-workplace-culture-2022-11-17/

Training Is Another Key

Beyond hiring, training is significant in building a successful practice and enforcing productivity. Training can be best understood by contrasting it with other educational pursuits, such as law school. While law school primarily imparts legal analytical capabilities, training focuses on applying these abilities to real-world legal matters involving individuals and businesses. This training can take various forms, including in-person sessions, online courses, and the incorporation of technology. It encompasses a wide array of skills, including legal expertise, client comprehension, effective communication, interpersonal skills, business acumen, billing procedures, time management, thorough preparation, ensuring confidentiality, information management, and more.

In the context of your firm, it's essential to determine your primary approach to training. Do partners predominantly take the lead in training new hires or is the responsibility primarily delegated to associates? Additionally, it's worth noting that California has instituted specific requirements for new attorney training since 2018, mandating that all newly admitted attorneys complete 10 hours of California Bar-approved training within their first year of bar admission, as stipulated in California Rules of Court, Rule 9.49.[10]

Training plays a critical role in optimizing productivity. Every member of a firm, spanning from trial attorneys to filing clerks, requires customized training to excel in their respective roles. Effective training significantly reduces errors, prevents unnecessary delays, and minimizes financial write-offs, thereby safeguarding profitability. Furthermore, well-trained staff members gain the confidence needed to handle both their current responsibilities and future challenges. As the staff become more proficient, they can better support the professional development of attorneys, contributing to higher attorney retention rates within the firm.

Furthermore, dedicating attention to training and delivering exceptional training experiences offers the added benefit of enhancing the law firm's overall reputation.

The Role of Mentorship

Effective mentorship enhances firm productivity. Successful mentorship involves the sharing of wisdom gained from experience. To be an effective mentor, one must commit personally and be willing to share, include

---

[10] https://www.calbar.ca.gov/Portals/0/documents/State-Bar-New-Attorney-Training-Program.pdf

others, communicate clearly, and set a positive example. Key qualities for mentors include patience, focus, realistic expectations, and providing encouragement. Good mentorship directly enhances productivity by offering professional guidance and feedback, facilitating the establishment of shared goals, and increasing attorney satisfaction.

For a successful mentor–mentee relationship, it is essential that a mentor doesn't serve as the direct supervisor of their mentee. This distinction allows the mentee the freedom to express vulnerability and acquire new knowledge without fearing performance judgments.

To build successful mentor relationships, mentors and mentees should schedule meetings outside of the firm to nurture their relationship and encourage open communication. Lunch often provides an excellent opportunity for this purpose. It offers a structured yet focused timeframe to address and discuss matters while also fostering rapport.

Productivity

All law firms utilize metrics to gauge productivity, which involves quantifying the performance of both lawyers and staff, regardless of their billing methods or practices. The primary objective for firms is to convert performance into revenue, as mentioned earlier. The ultimate goal shared by all firms is to boost their revenue streams.

Attorney productivity is assessed by calculating the amount of time, often billable, that can be charged to a client. This is commonly referred to as effective hours billed or utilization rate, and the higher this rate, the better. The realization rate, on the other hand, measures how much time an attorney spends on a task relative to the fees collected. A low realization rate is indicative of a problem, suggesting that an attorney is spending more time on tasks than can be billed to clients. This could be due to various factors such as write-offs, duplicated billing, inefficiencies, or delays.

Productivity begins with establishing clear expectations for partners in terms of their monthly and annual billable hour requirements. It's essential that partners, in line with the firm's practices, share the same obligations for billing hours as associate attorneys, even if the number of billable hours may differ. When these requirements are transparent, consistent, and adhered to, it can lead to increased productivity. It's important to note that monthly billable hours recorded on timesheets may not always directly correlate with the client's invoice. To calculate the "effective" hours billed or the utilization rate, one must compare the hours recorded on timesheets with the hours billed to the client. Simply put, the higher the percentage, the better. A solid target for effective hours billed is at least 90%. To improve the realization rate, it's crucial to identify the reasons behind write-offs. Typically, issues stem from either insufficient attorney training or client relations. Clients may resist the costs associated with necessary legal procedures or attorneys may operate inefficiently. This insight allows firms to focus their efforts on enhancing attorney training, refining client relations, or both.

What applies to professional staff at a law firm also holds true for non-professional staff. The first step is to make well-informed hiring decisions, followed by clearly defining roles and responsibilities and providing adequate training. Training not only contributes to success and job satisfaction but also reduces turnover, ultimately leading to increased productivity.

Profitability

When addressing attorney and staff productivity, the next concern is profitability. In general, a law firm's profitability is determined by subtracting total expenses from total revenue, calculated on a cash basis. To arrive at this figure, you start with the gross revenue, which includes all fees collected, and then subtract gross expenses, encompassing partner draws or W2 wages from any year-end wage statement. This resulting number reflects the overall law firm profitability. It's important to note that there is no specific percentage that defines success in profitability. One commonly used metric is "profits per partner," which involves dividing the overall profitability by the number of partners in the firm. However, this calculation can be somewhat misleading, as it can be manipulated based on the level of partner draws or salaries. Higher partner salaries or draws will result in lower profits. Tax matters will not be discussed here, as they are beyond the scope of this chapter.

To calculate profits, the first step is to calculate overhead expenses. Determine all law firm expenses paid within a 12-month period to establish the "overhead" (OH) figure. Then subtract partner draws, salaries, and any associated tax burdens. Next, subtract salaries for other professional staff, including associates, of-counsel, and paralegals, along with any tax burdens on their salaries. The result is the gross annual overhead expenses, which serves as the numerator. To determine the denominator, determine the full-time equivalents for professional staff. The formula becomes: numerator divided by denominator equals OH number, which is used for individual profitability calculations. Set forth as follows is an example of this calculation:

Law Firm, LLP

Overhead Calculation Based on Cash Basis Statement			**Annualized 2022**
Total Operating Expenses			$ 13,108,044
Less:			
Partners Salary			$ 4,902,143
Professional Staff			$ 2,681,165
Of Counsel			$ 4,938
Professional Staff Payroll Taxes (60%)			$ 201,635
Total Adjustments			$ 7,789,881
Total Overhead			$ 5,318,163
Numbers of Attorneys & Paralegals		**Full-time Equivalent**	
Attorneys			
Full Share	28.00	28.00	
Half Share	1.00	0.50	
Quarter Share	3.00	0.75	
Paralegals			
Full Share = 1/2 Share	4.00	2.00	
Half Share = 1/4 Share	0.00	0.00	
Total Shares			31.25
Overhead per Professional			$ 170,181

To calculate profitability by partner, start with the gross fee collections from all clients over a 12-month period (since partners typically generate work and should be measured based on collections, not billings like associates). Subtract the partner's total draw or salary (before any profits are paid) and then subtract the OH number. The resulting figure represents the profits generated by the partner before profit distribution. A target range for partner profitability is typically set at 25–33%. If a partner falls below this range, it's crucial to investigate the cause. Partners should ideally cover their draw, salary, and OH costs. Additionally, contributions to firm management duties, such as managing partner, executive committee member, practice group leader, or rainmaker, should be factored into their profitability assessment. Set out below is an example of this calculation:

PARTNER	**10/1/21 to 9/30/22**
Billable Hours	1,804
Non-Billable Hours	83
Total Hours	1,887
Fees Collected	$743,411
Draw	$171,750
Overhead	$170,181
Net Profit/Loss	$401,480
Profit Margin	54.00%

Associate profitability, on the other hand, it is calculated by determining the gross fee *billings* to all clients over a 12-month period, as associates are generally not responsible for collections within this timeframe. Subtract their total salary paid, any anticipated bonuses, and the OH number. The result indicates the profits generated by the associate. A desirable target range for associate profitability is 25–33%. If associates fall below this range, potential issues such as excessive write-offs or the need for more training and mentorship should be examined. Set out as follows is an example of this calculation:

ASSOCIATE	**10/1/21 to 9/30/11**
Billable Hours	1,650
Non-Billable Hours	177
Total Hours	1,827
Fees Billed	$475,047
Salary	$161,250
Overhead	$170,181
Y/E Bonus	TBD
Net Profit/Loss	$143,616
Profit Margin	30.23%

To calculate practice group profitability, the process begins with partners and associates separately. Partners' profitability involves gross fee *collections* from all clients over a 12-month period, while associates' profitability is based on their gross fee *billings* to all clients over the same timeframe. This allows for a comprehensive evaluation of each practice group's contribution to the firm's overall profitability. To calculate a practice group's profitability, you would need to repeat the calculations noted above for each partner and associate.

Financial Reporting: What Do We Really Need?

Each Day Is Important

To ensure the firm's partners effectively manage the firm's finances and achieve optimal results, it is crucial to maintain a high level of awareness regarding the firm's financial well-being. This necessitates daily monitoring of the financial health. For the successful operation of any business, it is imperative that the owners remain well-informed and vigilant in tracking cash flow. Specifically, the managing partner and all equity owners of the firm should be well-informed about which clients are making timely payments.

To facilitate this awareness, the head of the accounting department or accounting software should provide a daily report of total deposits by payee (e.g., client).

Monthly Reports[11]

Additionally, to promote transparency and awareness, it is advisable to prepare monthly financial statements, preferably by independent CPA firms using a "compiled" standard and cash and accrual basis accounting. These statements should be distributed to all partners. Furthermore, it is beneficial to include highlights in these reports to draw attention to trends, abnormal expenses, slow cash collections, and similar concerns.

Accounts Receivable Is About Accountability

Another vital aspect of financial management is the mandatory distribution of accounts receivable reports to all partners. These reports should include special notes regarding significant amounts and any problematic client issues. It is highly recommended to openly discuss these issues within the partnership group to collectively address them. Holding monthly partners meetings where financial information is distributed and discussed is an effective approach. These meetings should include a mandatory agenda item focusing on the overall financial health of the firm. This discussion should encompass cash flow, expense trends, and their management. It is crucial not to avoid addressing accounts receivable issues and, in fact, to be candid about challenging collection matters. This openness in communication is instrumental in establishing necessary action items for resolution.

Budgeting for Success

Law firms require budgets to determine appropriate compensation levels and are essential for the operation of all businesses. Budgets serve the crucial purpose of forecasting revenue and estimating expenses. Since all businesses have an inherent level of unpredictability, it's advisable to include a buffer or cushion in the budget. To effectively manage finances,

---

[11] For a definition of what "Compiled" Financial Statements are, see: https://us.aicpa.org/content/dam/aicpa/interestareas/privatecompaniespracticesection/qualityservicesdelivery/keepingup/downloadabledocuments/financial-statement-services-guide.pdf

it's essential to establish short-term benchmarks and a long-term strategy while closely monitoring cash flow.

Establishing an Annual Budget

1. **Fee Revenue:** Begin by incorporating fee revenue generated by attorneys and paralegals. Analyze the annual billed and collected hours over the past three years and multiply this by the expected billing rate (adjusting for planned increases). It's prudent to adopt a conservative approach. For contingency case revenue, only include it if the case is nearing resolution; otherwise, do not budget for anticipate cash fee revenue unless you are assured the fees will be realized in the budget year.
2. **Expense Review:** Thoroughly examine the firm's expenses, categorizing them accordingly. Utilize the monthly/annual financial statements for expense categories and make necessary adjustments for cost increases, such as salaries/draws, rent, vendor expenses, mailing, shipping, and don't forget to allocate funds for marketing. After finalizing the budget, share it with all partners for their review and approval. It's essential to note that budgets are not static; regular reviews are imperative. Conduct these reviews on a monthly or quarterly basis, comparing the budget to actual financial performance and addressing any variances promptly. Do not hesitate to adjust when needed.

Partnership Meetings

During partnership meetings, thoroughly discuss and analyze material variances in the budget. Partners should collectively determine the reasons behind these discrepancies.

Accountability and Partner Involvement

Budgets hold the firm and all partners accountable. Review all aspects of the budget mentioned above with all partners, seeking buy-in from each of them. Continuously discuss budget-related matters during periodic partner meetings. Establish action plans and assign responsibilities to partners while setting reporting deadlines (usually aligned with the next partner meeting, but it can be sooner).

Benchmark Discussion

Engage in discussions regarding benchmarks, covering areas such as attorney billings versus collections and the correlation between hours billed to clients and recorded on timesheets. Calculate the percentage of gross revenue collected and distributed to partners (using the profit calculation mentioned earlier and adding back draws/salaries) to determine the profit percentage. A return near 40% is considered a solid outcome for partners.

By adopting these practices, law firms can effectively utilize budgets to manage their financial affairs, ensure accountability among partners, and make informed decisions for the benefit of the organization.

Reports and Analysis as a Planning Tool

Cash Receipts Daily Report

As noted above, it is vitally important for leadership to monitor cash receipts daily. Further, the firm's accounting system or accounting department should report daily cash receipts to leadership and inform a partner when her or his client has paid. That way leadership can plan monthly and quarterly revenue and the timing of when expenses are to be paid.

Accounts Receivable Report—Monthly

At a minimum, each month the partner in charge of a client should receive a monthly report showing all outstanding invoices and that report should show how long each invoice has been outstanding (30 days, 60 days, 90 days or more). That way the partner, and firm leadership, can address which clients need to be approached to make payment and keep cash flow coming into the firm. Also, the firm can address if a client that owes substantial fees over an extended period of time is in financial distress and what steps the firm should take to minimize further financial exposure.

Monthly Fee Billing and Collection Report

Many accounting systems have the ability to provide, on a monthly basis, what each attorney (and paralegal) billed and collected for the previous month, and as the firm moves through the year, Year-To-Date (YTD) numbers. This report can be used to analyze the difference between what an attorney is each month (per the timesheets), what the firm billed to clients, and what was collected for the month. If leadership notices a material difference between the value of the fees to be billed per the timesheets versus the value of the fees billed to a client, leadership can address the root cause for any material difference. By way of example, is it because of a lack of efficiency (which may be lack of training), lack of direction by the partner on tasks completed, or is the lower amount billed to a client based on maintaining good client relationships? This analysis will then allow leadership to address the reason and take action.

Trust Account Deposits

In many states, firms have an affirmative obligation to return any unused trust account funds when a matter is over, or when the firm's relationship has ended. On a monthly basis, each partner should receive a trust account report stating the amount held in the trust account by client. Each partner in charge of a client should be obligated to review the report and make a determination whether the funds should be retained (under a previously executed retainer agreement) because the matter and the client are active, or returned since the matter is completed or the client relationship has ended. That way, the firm and the partner satisfy any state ethical obligations.

Billing, Receivables, and Collections

Electronic Billing

Electronic billing has become increasingly common, with clients utilizing various systems and interfaces. Gathering feedback regarding user-friendliness and identifying potential issues and communicating these issues with the platform manager is crucial.

Accounts Receivable(AR) Management

Effective management of receivables is vital for any firm's success, particularly in the case of law firms where accounts receivable collections serve as the financial lifeblood. To ensure success, it's imperative that the partner responsible for a client takes accountability for the collection process, and this commitment should be shared by all partners. Simplifying AR collections involves integrating features within the firm's accounting system that can identify accounts receivable exceeding 90 days outstanding (DOS). These flagged AR accounts should then be targeted for discussion, and decisions must be made on how to approach the client for payment.

The management of collections is a critical aspect of maintaining a firm's financial well-being. Collecting AR is the cornerstone of financial stability and is pivotal to the firm's overall fiscal health. In cases where firms may not have a dedicated Chief Financial Officer (CFO), the responsibility for this task falls on firm management and the partner with the primary client relationship. In some cases, firms can opt to enlist the assistance of external consultants for a nominal cost.

Billing Guidelines for Insurance Defense Practices

These guidelines can differ significantly from those of other types of firms, such as those engaged in criminal defense or strict contingency fee practices. In the context of insurance defense, it is essential for firms to obtain and thoroughly understand the billing guidelines before initiating any work. Furthermore, firms must ensure that their accounting department reviews and incorporates any limitations pertaining to billing, such as the specific costs that can and cannot be recovered. The partner overseeing the insurance client should also take the initiative to review the mandatory billing practices outlined in the guidelines and arrange training sessions for the attorneys involved. While billing guidelines have long been established in the insurance sector, a noteworthy industry trend is the emergence of large businesses issuing their own billing guidelines. Failing to adhere to these guidelines could result in non-payment for the services rendered, which would have detrimental consequences on multiple fronts.

Conclusion

The information shared in this chapter is not intended to be a full and complete analysis of how to run the financial aspects of a law firm. It is intended to start you on your journey to better gather financial information and use it to the benefit of the firm, partners, and all employees of your firm. They, like you, want a successful law firm family to "stay in business" and grow and prosper.

Chapter 10

Compensation Strategies for Law Firms

A Holistic Approach

Brian Kennel

Understanding market dynamics is crucial. Law firms must stay abreast of industry trends, including salaries, benefits, and perks offered by competitors. This knowledge enables them to position their compensation packages competitively and attract the best legal professionals. However, it is equally important to consider the firm's economics. Compensation structures should be sustainable and not jeopardize the firm's financial health.

Furthermore, cultural values play a significant role in shaping compensation decisions. Some firms prioritize egalitarianism, ensuring that all lawyers are compensated fairly and equitably. Others emphasize performance-based compensation, rewarding lawyers who generate the most revenue or achieve exceptional results. The firm's culture and values should guide the development of its compensation structure.

A well-rounded and holistic approach to compensation considers various factors beyond base salary. This includes benefits such as health insurance, retirement plans, and professional development opportunities. Additionally, firms may offer bonuses, profit-sharing, or equity partnership to incentivize lawyers and align their interests with the firm's success.

By embracing a strategic and well-rounded approach to compensation, law firms can position themselves for enduring success in an increasingly competitive legal landscape. They can attract and retain top talent, boost morale and productivity, and align their compensation practices with their broader strategic goals and values. Investing in a thoughtfully designed compensation structure is an investment in the firm's future and a testament to its commitment to excellence.

In the intricate tapestry of the legal profession, associate and partner compensation stands as a central thread, weaving together the aspirations of talented legal professionals, the economic heartbeat of law firms, and the intangible yet influential fabric of organizational culture. As law firms strive to attract, retain, and motivate top-tier talent, carefully calibrating compensation structures becomes paramount. This chapter explores the dynamics governing associate and partner compensation, emphasizing the pivotal roles played by market forces, firm economics, and organizational culture.

The Shifting Sands of Market Dynamics

A keen understanding of market dynamics lies at the heart of any effective compensation strategy. Legal professionals are skilled practitioners and discerning individuals who, armed with experience and expertise, actively assess their worth in the broader legal marketplace. Consequently, law firms must keep pace with the ever-evolving landscape of compensation trends, industry benchmarks, and competitive offerings.

Law firms must engage in a delicate dance with the market, where the compensation package becomes a significant determinant of success. By aligning associate and partner compensation with prevailing market standards, firms can position themselves as attractive employers, drawing in the best-fit legal minds. However, the challenge lies in meeting market expectations and ensuring the firm can discern which candidates best support the firm's strategic priorities.

Firm Economics: Beyond the Bottom Line

Market dynamics provide a compass, but a firm's economic health, intricately tied to its revenue streams, profitability, and financial stability, dictates its compensation boundaries.

Associates and partners alike are vital contributors to a firm's economic success, and their compensation should reflect not only the market's valuation of their skills but also the organization's financial realities. Maintaining a balance between rewarding individual and organizational contributions is also critical. This chapter will delve into the strategic considerations that law firms must navigate, offering insights into aligning compensation structures with the economic imperatives of the organization.

The Cultural Piece: Weaving Values into Compensation

Beyond numbers and financial metrics, a law firm's culture significantly influences how compensation is perceived and valued. An organization's culture, encompassing its values, ethics, and workplace dynamics, plays a pivotal role in shaping the attitudes of associates and partners toward their compensation.

A well-crafted compensation strategy should acknowledge individuals' contributions and reflect and reinforce the cultural principles that define the firm. This chapter unravels the intricate interplay between compensation and culture. It will guide law firms in aligning financial incentives with the intangible yet powerful forces that define their organizational identity.

As we work through the complexities of associate and partner compensation, it becomes evident that a successful strategy must be a harmonious blend of market responsiveness, economic pragmatism, and cultural resonance.

We promote a compensation best practices guide for law firms seeking to forge compensation structures that attract and retain exceptional talent and contribute to the organization's enduring success.

Associate Compensation Best Practices

Compensating associates is most often a complex undertaking. However, it is an annually recurring topic that law firms must address to attract and retain talent. We recommend approaching this process with a structure that anticipates trends and focuses on short-term needs and long-term goals. The following sections introduce some primary considerations and approaches law firms can use to create a well-rounded associate compensation plan.

Considerations

Associate compensation programs should factor in the following elements:

- Competitiveness: Compared to the market, how well are associates compensated at a firm, and where does the firm rank compared to its competitors?

- Progression: Does the firm have a consistent and progressive structure for raises and bonuses that aligns with its associates' experience and performance progress?
- Incentives: Does the firm incentivize behaviors that are aligned with its vision and priorities?
- Tenure: Does the plan incentivize staying with the firm and realizing its full potential?
- Transparency: How clear is the firm about the earning potential over time and at specific experience and performance levels?
- Feedback: Does the firm provide associates with sufficient performance feedback to draw a connection between their salary levels, raises and bonuses, and their performance?

Capacity and Performance Expectations

The first step when determining a compensation structure for attorneys is to look at their economic and qualitative capacity and capability now and in the future. We encourage law firms to determine expected performance levels or ranges for progressive contributions over the first eight to ten years of an attorney's career in the firm.

- Production Capacity: How much work will the attorney handle, and what is the value of that work? Production metrics may include billable hours or caseload, expected billings and collections, and, by extension, rates, and realization.
- Qualitative Performance: Which skills does the attorney need to succeed in the position/ to create value? Consider legal skills, case management, business development contributions, compliance/ interpersonal skills, recruiting support, etc.
- Profitability: How much economic value should the attorney create beyond their cost? (Expected profit dollars and profit margin %)

The qualitative increases in value and objective contributions to revenue and profit indicated in the table that follows provide an example of the most common factors. It is helpful to consider contributions in the context of those increasing long-term value and offering short-term profits.

Increases in Value	Contributions to Profit
Quality of professional work	Personal productivity
Work ethic (consistency of quality and quantity)	Profitability of others (supervision and training)
Client relationships and service	Originations
Personal development, accountability, and timely skills and business maturity progression	Recruiting profitable lawyers
Business development contributions (networking, publishing, speaking, etc.)	Business hygiene (timekeeping, billing, collections)
Cultural support	
Firm building (recruiting, training, process development, etc.)	
Adding to the (brand) reputation of the firm	

This table indicates an example of expectations by experience level.

PERFORMANCE EXPECTATIONS	
KEY	Consistent
	Approaching consistent
	Optional
	Not expected at the experience level

ECONOMIC FACTORS						
Experience (YR)	Productivity	Realization	Training Supervision	Profit Threshold	Billing Management	Origination
1						
2						
3						
4						
5						
6						
7						
8						
9						
10						

QUALITATIVE FACTORS - WEALTH CREATION								
Experience (YR)	Work Ethic	Work Quality	Bar, Professional Civic	Content Publishing Speaking	Business Development Competence	Recruiting Contributions	Client Relations and Service	Pro Bono
1								
2								
3								
4								
5								
6								
7								
8								
9								
10								

A firm may combine economic scores and consider the aggregate result as a single qualitative factor. As long as the selected system is consistently applied, room exists for customization.

Designing a compensation strategy that maximizes your law firm's legal workforce's value is critical. It requires thoughtful consideration of various factors, including economic scores and qualitative measures. By finding the right balance and customizing your approach, your firm can attract and retain top lawyers while nurturing a consistent organizational culture.

To start, it is crucial to clearly define the skill set that brings long-term value to your firm. Identifying the qualities contributing to success and appropriately compensating your lawyers based on these factors will ensure you retain the best-fit individuals who can help your firm flourish.

One effective tactic is to reward lawyers who consistently excel in high-value categories such as work ethic, work quality, and client service. By recognizing their exceptional performance and moving them into higher salary bands, you motivate them to continue delivering impressive results.

For firms with top lawyers approaching retirement, creating a compensation system that encourages future stars to step up and assume leadership roles is essential. By offering incentives and flexibility, you ensure a smooth transition while nurturing the continued success of your organization.

It is also necessary to acknowledge the value of specialized expertise and reward it accordingly. For example, if trial experience is highly valued in your litigation firm, compensating successful litigators who excel in this area is an excellent strategy. Finally, recognizing qualitative accomplishments, such as publishing high-quality content, can motivate your lawyers to contribute to the firm's mission.

A well-designed compensation strategy that considers both qualitative and economic performance is critical to motivating and retaining the best-fit individuals for your law firm. By going beyond base salary increases and acknowledging the contributions that go above and beyond, you ensure the fairness and success of your organization.

Setting Compensation Ranges—Building a 10-year Associate Pay Scale Model

When setting base salaries, the best approach to creating a salary scale begins with considering economic (internal and external COLA), qualitative performance expectations, and comparative market salary data (when reliable and available). Combining these internal and external elements into an associate pay scale model that spans ten years will ensure the firm's associate pay remains market competitive and economically sustainable when factored into the firm's long-range financial model.

Determining a Target Base Salary Progression

Communicating how meeting performance expectations will impact an attorney's pay is essential. Again, we recommend building this out considering the following factors for the first ten years of experience:

1. Using the best available data, determine the market pay rate for associates at each year of experience.
2. Plug a draft salary progression into your associate compensation model using a first-year baseline, including profitability (Cash and Billed). We suggest an annual compensation escalator of the CPI plus market adjustments, tenure, and merit. The market adjustment may indirectly account for merit, so keep that in mind.
3. Set objective and subjective performance benchmarks.
4. Ensure your model includes target working attorney billings and collections, benchmark billing rates, and realization at various experience levels.
5. Identify target profitability at each level.
6. Compare the remainder to the projected overhead per lawyer at each level.
7. Compare the amount remaining to cover overhead.
8. Consider if the associate pay scale is competitive and economically viable.
9. Revise the various levers that include hours, rates, realization, and overhead costs.

Once the target salary progression model is satisfactory, firms can define a minimum/maximum salary range for years 1–10. Set salaries between the minimum and maximum for each experience year so higher raises and salaries can account for merit and tenure without busting the salary scale.

Overhead Policies

Accurate profitability calculation requires overhead allocations, which often require a degree of subjectivity to determine. We prefer a graduated method of allocating overhead that affords young attorneys sufficient time to grow their billing and realization rates. Additionally, attorneys who are not partners may have some influence over direct legal assistant support costs; they generally have minimal control over the firm's remaining overhead expenditures. As a result, they rely on firm management and the partners to ensure efficient overhead cost management. With our preferred approach, the result of inefficient overhead management rests with the equity partners.

The allocation of overhead costs varies from firm to firm and is characterized by different shares assigned to each timekeeper type based on experience level, although some firms assign it evenly.

Here is a sample of a progressive overhead allocation structure we use.

Allocated Overhead Conventions

Timekeeper Type	Experience Level	Indirect Overhead Allocation Share
Equity Member/Partner	All	Full Share
Income Partner	All	75–100% of an equity member's share
Senior Associate	6+	65% of an equity member's share
Associate	1–5 years	50% of an equity member's share
Paralegal	All	25% of an equity member's share

Items Included in Overhead

Two types of allocated overhead include directly allocated costs and generally allocated costs. The allocated overhead conventions refer only to general overhead expenses.

Direct Overhead Costs

Directly allocated overhead costs consist primarily of legal assistant (secretarial) payroll costs and benefits. Directly allocating legal assistant (secretarial) costs to each lawyer incents sharing and introduces a measure of accountability into legal assistant (secretarial) use. For example, attorneys who use legal assistants efficiently enable more sharing among other lawyers and positively impact profitability-based bonus formulas (reduced direct overhead increases timekeeper profit). Alternatively, attorneys not efficiently using legal assistant (secretarial) resources will limit sharing opportunities, resulting in a higher direct overhead allocation.

While direct overhead allocations primarily include legal assistant (secretarial) resources, attorneys may receive direct shares of clerical and other support resource costs.

It is possible to allocate other costs that do not benefit the common good directly.

Generally Allocated Overhead Costs

Generally allocated overhead includes all remaining costs after deducting timekeeper pay and benefits, legal assistant (secretarial) pay and benefits, and other direct resource cost and expense allocations. Law firms typically group expenses into the following areas:

- Salaries and Benefits
- Facility Costs
- Equipment and Practice Aids
- Practice Development
- General and Administrative

A full explanation of these areas is beyond what is necessary here.

Discretionary Overhead Exclusions

Management must retain some discretion over the application of overhead. Exclusions may include extraordinary expenses that would unfairly affect profitability. Adjust overhead allocations to reflect each timekeeper's full-time equivalency and any special adjustments for approved leave or partial-year performance.

Managing Base Compensation

Law firms that employ strategic approaches to base compensation to foster professional growth and set base compensation have advantages. By understanding the dynamics of qualitative progression and the impact of billable and non-billable time investments, law firms can create a rewarding and sustainable career path for lawyers. Here is an explanation of the key factors influencing base salaries and the importance of supporting non-billable activities.

1. Qualitative Progression and Early Career Enhancements: Typically, lawyers experience faster and more pronounced qualitative improvements earlier in their careers. The progression largely depends on their skills, initiative, access to training, and the complexity of their work. Law firms must ensure ample professional development and skill enhancement opportunities to facilitate this growth.
2. Billable Hours and Learning Curve: Meeting billable hours requirements financially rewards lawyers and the firm and can contribute to a shorter learning curve. These investments in billable time allow lawyers to hone their expertise and gain valuable experience.

3. Non-Billable Time Investments for Long-Term Value: Unlike billable hours, non-billable time investments require a similar commitment but typically do not lead to short-term profits. Instead, non-billable investments should lead to long-term value that stays with the lawyer throughout their career. Law firms should demonstrate a genuine interest in their lawyers' long-term success by supporting valuable non-billable activities.
4. Evolving Compensation Programs: Base salaries tend to increase rapidly during the early stages of a lawyer's career but eventually plateau or even transition into other incentive programs. Originations and profitability-sharing opportunities become key criteria for compensation, especially for more senior lawyers. For example, a share of the profits generated by attorneys under the supervision of a more senior lawyer.

By recognizing the dynamics of qualitative progression, supporting non-billable activities, and implementing strategic compensation programs, law firms can empower lawyers to achieve professional growth and financial success. A well-designed compensation structure attracts good lawyers and ensures long-term career sustainability.

Adjusting Base Salaries

Determining base salary adjustments requires careful consideration of progressive economic and qualitative performance expectations relative to actual performance. To ensure a fair and transparent process, consider the following:

Evaluators should consider economic performance indicators such as production, profitability, and supervision (maximizing production of others). Additionally, they should consider qualitative performance factors such as skills, work ethic, business development, administrative contributions, and mentorship.

In the early phases of an attorney's career, emphasize qualitative contributions when making base salary decisions. It is essential to cultivate well-rounded professionals who excel in their legal skills and broader impact on the firm.

As attorneys progress and master their legal skills, the significance of economic performance increases. We augment expertise with greater weight on monetary contributions. Creating valuable skills should result in financial rewards for the firm and the lawyer.

The ultimate goal is to foster an environment that rewards high engagement and excellence. By aligning base salaries and increases with evolving expectations, we encourage attorneys to realize their full potential qualitatively and economically.

1. Raise structure:
2. Generally speaking, the two types of raise structures are lockstep and balanced. Law firms sometimes default to lockstep systems for determining base salaries, especially for lawyers in the first 5–7 years of practice. Using a "pass-fail" approach to determine base salary increases, a lockstep approach gives salary increases commensurate with rank to those lawyers who have done enough to progress. Poorly performing lawyers do not advance. This approach fails to consider lawyers who may not warrant a maximum salary increase but have done enough to earn something. Since the class year is the primary salary determination, lockstep approaches tend to have poor evaluation systems. It is easy to see why top performers feel frustrated and unmotivated under this approach. To mitigate some of the negative aspects of this approach, firms may use lockstep to recognize differences in learning curves. In this instance, the idea is that it is more important that a lawyer is progressing and their absolute place compared to their peers is less critical. Eventually, everyone catches up, or they must leave.
3. A better approach is to set salary ranges for each year with a balanced approach and determine raises based on progressive expectations for economic performance and qualitative contributions, as explained in the previous sections. To evaluate the raises systematically, consider the following process:
4. First, determine performance bands for the economic and qualitative factors (e.g., if the billable hour target is 1600, consider three bands: 1500–1599, 1600–1699, and 1700 plus). Each band should receive a score (e.g., three bands: 1, 2, 3). Then consider weighing the contributions by experience level, for example:

    - Years 1–3: Economic/ Qualitative 33/67
    - Years 4–6; Economic/ Qualitative 50/50
    - Years 7–10: Economic/ Qualitative 67/33

5. Each attorney receives a score based on where their performance falls in each performance component. See this evaluation table example:
6. Raise amount:

ECONOMIC FACTORS			
Factor	**Minimum (1)**	**At Target (2)**	**Above Target (3)**
Productivity (Billable Hours/ Cases Contributed)			
Realization (Billings & Collections)			
Profit threshold			
Billing management			
Origination			
Composite Score			

QUALITATIVE FACTORS			
Factor	**Minimum (1)**	**At Target (2)**	**Above Target (3)**
Work Ethic			
Work Quality			
Bar, Professional, and Civic			
Marketing Contributions			
Skill Development			
Training and supervision			
Recruiting contributions			
Client relations and service			
Pro Bono			
Composite Score			

7. Determine the actual raise by applying the attorney's raise score to the salary range for the upcoming year (the higher the score, the closer the raise to the upper salary range limit). Consider here the following aspects:
    - Cover at least the average inflation rate (BLS CPI)—additional merit raises based on performance scores
    - Calculate future capacity (how much do you expect the attorney to produce next year?)
    - Allocate raises (according to evaluation factors and market pay rate)
    - Project payroll increases for the upcoming year

The raise process reduces turnover and ensures that best-fit lawyers thrive. However, to keep this process efficient and incentivize the right behaviors, we encourage firms to develop a systematized approach like the one we introduced here. Firms should work toward publishing expectations and salary ranges to their employees while applying the evaluation system during their raise discussions. Remember that the keys to an effective system include transparency in performance targets and earnings and a consistent process.

Law Firm Bonus Strategies: A Guide to Compensating Attorneys

Compensating attorneys is a combination of art and science. Bonus plans are integral to most law firm compensation plans at all levels. Here is an overview of law firms' various bonus strategies to compensate attorneys, including advantages, disadvantages, and selection considerations.

1. Defined amount over a threshold (x $ per hour over the billable goal)
2. Percentage of salary as a bonus based on simple pass/fail criteria
3. Percentage of fees over the threshold: collections, billings, etc. (set expected production levels and give out a percentage of collections/ billings over the threshold as a bonus)
4. Predefined bonus pool split among eligible lawyers (define a pool and divide between eligible lawyers, which can be tiered based on seniority or other factors)
5. Profitability bonus (percentage of collections over a certain profit threshold, e.g., 15% of individual profitability over $75,000)
6. Profit-sharing pool (monthly, quarterly, semi-annual, or annual share of firm profit- individual shares can be tiered based on seniority or other factors)
7. Origination bonus (incentivize business development by giving origination credit for originated files/ clients)
8. Evaluation with points-based allocation of bonuses in tiers (points for economic and qualitative contributions and bonus dollar tiers for point ranges). This one functions similarly to the balanced raise structure we introduced earlier. In this case, the firm determines a dollar value for points ranges on the economic and qualitative performance level scale. The maximum payout can be structured with a progressive increase, assuming that performance improves with experience so that associates can improve their bonus payouts year over year with higher economic and qualitative contributions.

Choosing the right bonus plan depends on the firm culture and the behaviors the firm wants to incentivize. A simple dollar reward for meeting the billable hour target is easy to calculate and rewards billable productivity; however, it ignores qualitative contributions like legal skill improvements or helping with marketing campaigns. A team-based reward, like a shared bonus pool, is excellent for group performance, but if the firm has a few overachievers, they may feel underappreciated. Each system has pros and cons; ultimately, the firm must assess which system fits their organization best. However, a combination of salary increases and bonuses that capture and reward economic and qualitative performance is necessary to ensure long-term success.

Combining Salary and Bonus

When putting salary and bonus together, law firms often consider their philosophy on the incentive structure as follows:

Higher Base/ Lower Bonus	Base salaries closer to the top of the applicable range and typical bonuses ranging from 5–10% of salary or less
Lower Base/ Higher Bonus	Base salaries are lower than the market average, but typical bonuses can range as high as 20% of compensation for high-producers

While the lower base approach reduces the financial risk of underperformers, it can harm a law firm's competitiveness in the labor market. Over the last five years, base salary levels seemed to receive the most weight from attorneys when deciding to join or stay with a firm. While other factors, such as work environment and career opportunities, receive some consideration, attributing dollar values to them is difficult. Base compensation provides certainty and financial security to help meet rising living expenses and debt service.

A balanced compensation approach proves most valuable, as it includes modeling to help the firm forecast its financial position at different salary levels and bonus payouts for its associates. Law firms can model their attorneys' future capacity, overhead, and billing rates to estimate how anticipated raises and bonuses impact their profitability.

While market conditions constantly change and each firm's economic model differs, some historical benchmark values may help firms establish their initial salary progression structures.

Recommended Initial Comp Ranges (as % of billings/ collections)*:

0–3 Years	4–7 Years	8+ Years
25%-30%	30%-35%	35%-40%

* These ranges are considered only for working attorney performance. As attorneys mature, they may take on additional responsibilities that could justify an expansion of these ranges in later years.

Typical Minimum Profit Margin Ranges

Year 1	Year 2	Year 3	Year 4	Year 5	Year 6	Year 7	Year 8	Year 9	Year 10
0–15%	20%	20–30%	25–35%	30–40%	35–45%	35–40%	30–40%	15–30%	10–30%

Disclaimer: specific values depend on firm size, practice areas, billing rates, overhead structure, and firm lifecycle stage (startup, growth, maturity, decline)

While the high base approach is more competitive in today's associate market, law firms should consider increasing the risk-based portion of the compensation over time (gradual transition from higher base/lower bonus to lower base/higher bonus), especially once advanced attorneys hit a production ceiling and need to contribute value in other ways, such as training younger associates, developing new business, and participating in firm management.

Three Essential Elements of Equity Owner Compensation Systems

Equity owner compensation is a complex topic, with different systems often depending on firm size, structure, practice type, and culture. These income allocation systems can range from a simple profit split based on ownership percentages to more intricate processes involving weights and measures analyzed over varying intervals. All law firms can benefit from considering the best practices discussed as follows.

Key Metrics: Originated Fees and Working Attorney Fees

Merit-based systems heavily emphasize personal accountability and typically rely on two key metrics: originated fees (gross or net profit) and working attorney gross fees or profit. Other valuable objective factors exist, such as supervised fees (fees managed) or hours invested in training, but often do not receive the same consideration as working and originating performance.

Framework: Objective and Subjective Systems

Law firms often employ objective or subjective systems to determine compensation. Objective systems use metrics and data to arrive at awards, while subjective systems rely on the judgment and evaluations of senior leadership or peers. Both systems have their pros and cons, and the type of system a firm employs is often dictated by firm culture, practice type, firm size, talent market, strategic priorities, and firm age demographics.

Transparency: Open and Closed Systems

The level of transparency in compensation systems varies greatly among law firms. While open systems provide full disclosure of how compensation is calculated for each partner, closed systems generally only inform individual partners about their awards. Each approach has pros and cons, but all systems must measure the right factors, employ a fair process, and produce fair outcomes that will stand up in the market.

Emerging Trends in Law Firm Compensation

In recent years, the legal industry has witnessed significant generational changes and trends that have caused law firms to rethink compensation practices. One notable shift is the increasing focus on work-life balance and the recognition of non-originating partners' contributions. Law firms feel pressure to expand the factors that impact compensation and reward operational excellence, team management, a broader definition of profitability, and a more robust set of subjective contributions that we refer to as wealth creation.

Challenges and the Need for Evolution

The cultural shift in attitudes toward partnership has also created challenges for law firms concerning adding new equity owners. Increased turnover and a desire for a more balanced and collaborative approach to practicing law have made it difficult for firms to pass on from generation to generation, and many talented lawyers do not necessarily want the responsibility and risk accompanying equity ownership. Law firm compensation systems must adapt to these changing expectations by offering robust incentives and long-term benefits.

Developing a Compensation System

The same principles and best practices apply to any equity owner compensation framework, whether objective, subjective, open, or closed. The essential elements of a sound compensation system include the following:

- A fair and consistent process
- Setting appropriate expectations
- Reward value creation and innovation
- Attractive long-term incentives

Considering these elements, law firms will be better equipped to develop and maintain a successful partner compensation system.

Partner compensation is complex, but understanding how it works is essential for any law firm's success. By recognizing best practices, adjusting to emerging trends, and developing fair systems for current and prospective equity owners, firms can create a system that sets them up for long-term success.

Ensuring Alignment with Key Characteristics of the Firm

Aligning equity owner compensation systems with a firm's lifecycle stage and strategic objectives is recommended. Consider the following factors:

Lifecycle Stage

Is the firm a recent startup that needs to generate cash quickly? Is the firm in growth mode, or has it already matured? Is the firm declining and requires a reboot to change its current trajectory? Assessing the firm's lifecycle state is essential in building an effective compensation strategy.

Strategy

What is the firm's long-term vision and strategy, and is the compensation plan aligned with the goals? Are immediate changes necessary to ensure equity owners remain confident in the firm's future? Is the firm growing and needs equity owner participation in organizational development? Gaining consensus in a strategy to achieve the firm's goals and aligning compensation to incent necessary behaviors is optimal. Too many firms have misalignment in their compensation systems and strategic goals.

Values and Environment

Is the firm's compensation plan supposed to foster a collaborative approach or reward individual performance? Building consensus around the firm's culture and values also contributes to the success of a compensation strategy. Ensure the firm creates a compensation plan that aligns with the firm's stated values.

Examples of Typical Equity Owner Compensation Plans;

- Salary + Bonus (typically used for income partners): This is an extension of the associate compensation structure. Raises and bonuses continue to be based on progressive expectations. However, at this point, incentive-based compensation increases and bonus opportunities increase. Bonus options include salary percentages (e.g., up to 10% of salary for different contribution categories), percentage of fees collected or originated, percentage of fees managed, or a points-based system.
- Formula: The eat-what-you-kill system incentivizes individual performance for originating, managing, and producing fees. It is sometimes supplemented with additional bonus categories that reward qualitative contributions.
- Draw and Profit/Ownership Interest Share: Some firms may simply share profits according to ownership percentages, which works when there is a consensus that every partner's economic and qualitative contributions more or less match their ownership share.
- Lockstep: Setting compensation by seniority. Sometimes, firms create bonus pools for a fraction of the net profit each year to recognize outstanding contributions.

Most equity owner compensation systems contain elements of one of these basic approaches. Law firms like to create hybrid models that allow flexibility when paying partners. The freedom to modulate compensation based on evolving factors is tempting but comes with significant risks. Consistency and predictability rank high among the factors that make equity owner compensation systems effective. Introduce subjectivity and inconsistency at your peril.

Law Firm Equity Owner Compensation Framework and Approach

Any sound law firm's equity owner compensation system includes rewards for **Income Generation, Wealth Creation, Management, and Capital** (Investing in the firm). Within these areas, specific contributions exist and correlate to high-impact behaviors that break into objective and subjective contributions. We'll review the expected objective contributions, which should inform equity owner compensation awards.

Income and Profit Generation

There are four, and sometimes five, prominent roles in generating income and profit. These roles, discussed next, include the Originator, Client Relationship Manager, Workload Manager, Working Attorney, and sometimes Subject Matter Experts.

Bringing the Client in (ORIGINATOR)

Attracting new clients is a demanding undertaking that involves expertise and dedication. We have observed that only approximately 20% of lawyers in the private sector do what is necessary to secure new clients consistently. Since most law firms depend on rainmakers to sustain their functions, it is essential to reward origination contributions adequately. Originator pay varies, but in lateral transactions, the market usually pays 15%–25% of gross fee collection from the originator's files—the variation in the compensation range relates to billing rates, staffing, and, by extension, profitability.

Firms that use profitability-based systems would convert to an equivalent percentage of net income from the clients or files.

Law firms increasingly recognize the risks associated with highly concentrated origination practices and have expanded compensation awards to incentivize robust participation in business development. Firms that use system-based marketing focused on building business for a team or the firm's brand will need expanded incentives to encourage attorneys to support the system (content generation, speaking, professional networks, etc.). An in-depth discussion of clients' changing buying behavior is more than we have time for now. Still, law firms can realize significant benefits by revamping their marketing systems and incentives to meet these evolving priorities.

Managing the Client Relationship at the File Level (CLIENT/FILE MANAGER)

Lawyers who independently work and manage files directly with client personnel deserve some share of the credit. In many firms, these efforts go unrecognized, and expanding incentives would help improve morale and client service. In the same light, lawyers who manage case assignments they did not originate must handle these clients as if they originated them. Assuming this basic bargain is satisfied, we suggest the client/file lawyer receive up to 20% of the credit (credit is not synonymous with gross fees; it is more akin to profit or a formula credit) in the reward system.

No credit sharing is necessary if the originator works and manages the client's files. However, there are instances where the originating lawyer brings in the client but depends on another lawyer to handle the files. Most firms distinguish between non-owner lawyers and equity owners when sharing the client/file credit. Some firms begin to share client/file credit and the related benefits when an associate is promoted to a non-equity partner. Equity owners who manage client relationships for another equity owner typically receive some credit, as much as 80% in some instances.

Most firms that use formula-based compensation systems only consider working attorney production and origination when allocating the objective portion of the compensation. Due to formula constraints, client/file credit is often treated as an origination credit. Some claim that referring to client/file management as an origination credit is a misnomer, but it matters less if the appropriate recognition is understood and credit is received.

Managing Other Timekeepers (WORKLOAD MANAGER)

Managing timekeepers is another essential element of creating profit in a law firm. Managing workload distribution and optimizing production efficiency is challenging. It is typical for originating lawyers to manage the client relationship and timekeepers, but as they grow, they must enlist the help of others. While less prevalent, recognizing the role of the workload manager is essential. We suggest timekeeper management is worth up to 20% of the credit in the reward system. If the same lawyer manages the client/file relationship and manages the timekeepers, they could earn up to 40% of the credit in the reward system. Recently, we introduced a Fes Managed metric into our recommended compensation systems.

Working the File and Providing Legal Services (WORKER/ PRODUCER)

The credit described here would inform a partner's performance award if a firm's compensation system includes a working attorney compensation pool. Production credit is the dollar value of the revenue received from a partner's production. For example, if a partner records $10,000 in time dollar value, billed and collected, they would receive a $10,000 production credit (if the firm uses profitability instead of gross, use that number).

Overwhelmingly, non-owner (employees with W2 status) lawyers receive a base salary and a bonus for their efforts as working attorneys. Hourly and contract lawyers often receive a share of their fees or an amount per hour. Production, experience, and expertise are the factors that hold the most weight when compensating working attorneys. Most equity owners also receive pay for working attorney production, but it is typically through a compensation system that may or may not directly attribute pay to timekeeping.

Market pay for working attorney contributions can range from 25% to 40% of the gross fees from their work. To compare your compensation structure for non-owner lawyers to the market, arrange your salaries by bar year (experience) and compare them to these ranges. Compensation should generally scale with expertise and consistent performance. To reduce turnover, consider tenure. Almost every firm has exceptions, but we encourage firms to examine any inconsistencies objectively. Finally, these are only ranges, and we recommend law firms balance market benchmarks with their compensation strategy and economic model.

Equity owner-working attorney compensation may not easily translate into these ranges, and firm profitability will dictate how much compensation is available for equity owners. These market-based percentages are a reasonable guide for judging the competitiveness of your firm's compensation results.

Subject Matter Experts

Compensating subject matter experts is complicated. For example, if the firm invests in developing an attorney's technical expertise, an originator could argue that no origination credit is necessary if they introduce the subject matter expert to a client. While this is technically true, it is essential to consider where not sharing could lead. If the subject matter expert bonds with the client and becomes a go-to resource, you incentivize them to leave and take that portion of the client's work to their new firm by not sharing the success with the subject matter expert. Why do that? We recommend sharing the success and continuing to build on it. We believe denying origination (or other credit if the system allows it) is short-sighted.

Credit allocation depends on whether the subject matter expert functions in the other roles described above. However, pure subject matter expertise could draw between 20% and 50% of the credit.

Final Thoughts

If you feel that all of these considerations deliver a complexity that is hard to administer, you'll have a lot of company. Still, getting equity owner compensation right is essential, and a sound system can make all the difference. With the right combination of data, tools and analysis, transparency, and objectivity, well-reasoned compensation awards become much more accessible.

Compensating for Subjective Contributions from Law Firm Equity Owners: Wealth Creation (Organizational Development)

Often, the most significant contributions to a firm's long-term competitive advantage are not recognizable as immediate economic contributions. One example is recruiting a lawyer who eventually earns admission to equity ownership. Indeed, other valuable contributions facilitated the lawyer's success, but it typically starts with a well-executed recruiting strategy. To properly understand the value of subjective donations, we suggest thinking of them as wealth-creation activities that add value to the firm over longer durations. The essential wealth creation factors we suggest considering in your firm's compensation system include:

- Recruiting
- Attorney Training and Development
- Branding and Marketing
- Systems and Intellectual Property
- Management
- Cultural Development

We suggest designating 10–40% of the firm's profit, using the type of firm, lifecycle stage, strategic goals, and profitability to guide how much to apportion to wealth creation. What follows is a more detailed approach to valuing each factor.

Law Firm Recruiting Contributions: What Are the Key Performance Indicators, and How Do You Reward Them?

Law firms almost always underappreciate the effort to recruit talented attorneys and staff. Considering that the difference in most law firms' success is their people's quality and dedication, recognizing recruiting contributions should rank near the top of the awards list. Recruiting contributions fall into that category that we call wealth creation, which includes a group of subjective contributions. Compensating for wealth creation is accomplished by balancing the profit allocated to objective and subjective pools. For example, after carefully reviewing its economic needs and strategic goals, a firm allocates 70% of its net income to economic performance and 30% to wealth creation. Firms can modulate these amounts to correlate with their strategic and financial needs. Recruiting is a wealth creation factor and would receive a share of the net income allocated to the subjective factors.

Also, most law firms, especially larger ones, employ a lateral hiring strategy to fuel growth, increase profit, or add expertise. Some do it well, while others try and fail. In search of immediate success and using narrow criteria, many go to the "free agent market" to find seasoned attorneys with more significant books of business. If a firm has money to spend and can pay headhunter fees, finding lateral candidates is not tricky but expensive. We're not talking about compensating for these efforts here.

We recommend rewarding contributions to the firm's overall recruiting effectiveness and consistency. We also recommend building key performance indicators (KPIs) using criteria that include candidate identification (search), interviewing and vetting, brand building, peer recruiting, law school programs, internal committees, and organizing and managing recruiting events.

The list below includes several KPIs that a firm can easily measure, indicating the recruiting program's effectiveness and its operators.

- Quality candidates identified and interviewed
- Quality candidates hired compared to the target
- Targeted law school hires against the target
- Number of laterals recruited internally
- Colleague recruiting
- Number of employable candidates from social media outreach
- Targeted attendance at recruiting events
- Awards and accomplishments related to best places to work

With a little effort, a firm can create additional or better KPIs for their firm. It is much easier to conduct subjective performance evaluations if comparative data exists. Recruiting is the lifeblood of thriving firms, and fully appreciating the effort it takes to attract and retain quality attorneys staff can have the same return on investment as new business development.

Compensating for Wealth Creation: Attorney Training and Development

Increased turnover due to the hot lateral hiring market, aging lawyers, and increased attractiveness of in-house positions have created a significant need for attorney training and development. Shortstaffed law firms must rely on senior lawyers to handle client work, which leaves little time for training and development. These factors contribute to a need for more attention to developing younger lawyers for future positions on client teams, firm leadership, and management, making a law firm vulnerable to declining revenues and profitability.

Many firms need discernible incentives for training and mentoring in their compensation plans. However, many believe it is a duty or in one's self-interest to train lawyers who can make partners money and enable practice growth. We think this is oversimplified and results in inconsistent training and development firm-wide. For example, if an attorney is fortunate enough to work for a partner who is also a good trainer, the likelihood of future success is much greater.

If a firm is trying to build a solid brand that benefits more people, a formal attorney training and mentoring program is necessary, supported by incentives in the compensation plan. Recognizing that a good training and mentoring program will shorten the time for new attorneys to reach profitability is paramount and measurable.

Attorney development contributions fall into that category that we call wealth creation, which includes a group of subjective contributions. Compensating for wealth creation is accomplished by balancing the profit allocated to objective and subjective pools. For example, after carefully reviewing its economic needs and strategic goals, a firm allocates 70% of its net income to economic performance and 30% to wealth creation. Firms can modulate these amounts to correlate with their strategic and financial needs. Attorney development is a wealth creation factor and would receive a share of the net income allocated to the subjective factors.

The essential tools and performance indicators related to training and development include:

- Written training plans and assignments
- Written practice plans
- Evaluation and feedback systems
- Creation and monitoring of progression criteria
- Attorney progress metrics

- Turnover statistics
- Attorney realization and profitability

Evidence of the work in these areas creates a basis for compensation awards, including tracking the progress of younger lawyers for the first 7–10 years of experience and time with the firm.

Compensating for Law Firm Wealth Creation: Marketing and Brand Development

Marketing and brand development draw the most attention in law firm equity owner compensation systems' evaluation of non-economic contributions. Some compensate for the effort, and others believe that origination rewards effectively compensate for marketing. Some also believe the firm's monetary support for marketing expenditures is reward enough.

While in line with mainstream compensation practices in law firms, these concepts narrowly define business development as new or existing business procurement and maintenance success, not efforts. Attributing origination credit to shared situations is often tricky. The current approach to law firm marketing and the associated rewards is evolving. In our experience, the younger lawyers are more willing to share credit and collaborate on managing client relationships. Cynically, this is sometimes described as lacking drive or a willingness to pay the price of success. We'll see how the next ten years shape up, but many senior lawyers who control large business books will age out, and the business they so tightly controlled for their careers will return to the market.

Alert law firms understand they have to compete in today's world but also invest in initiatives that build the strength of their client offerings for longer durations. They allocate significant time and money to branding and collaborative marketing activities designed to create value in their organizations. These firms realize that many of today's superstar business developers and lawyers will either retire or often leave, and a strong brand with a solid reputation can help offset these losses.

Compensating for branding and marketing activities in the context discussed here relates to increasing the firm's name recognition and prestige for the benefit of everyone. Firms that enjoy strong brand recognition in the marketplace and invest in activities to grow and increase the effectiveness of this recognition provide a platform and level of prestige that makes individual marketing efforts more effective.

Branding and marketing contributions fall into that category that we call wealth creation, which includes a group of subjective contributions.

Compensating for wealth creation is accomplished by balancing the profit allocated to objective and subjective pools: for example, after carefully reviewing its economic needs and strategic goals, a firm allocates 70% of its net income to economic performance and 30% to wealth creation. Firms can modulate these amounts to correlate with their strategic and financial needs. Branding and marketing is a wealth creation factor and would receive a share of the net income allocated to the subjective factors.

As a starting point, here are the KPIs and process tools to support these longer-term branding and marketing efforts

- Planning and strategy development
    - ❒ Written firm and individual marketing plans
- Content contributions to the firm's digital presence
    - ❒ Articles, podcasts, blogs, and video participation, website contributions
- Participation in and generating for others high profile speaking engagements
    - ❒ Key industry conferences, client-centric events, legal networking events
- Referral network sharing
    - ❒ Sharing referral networks with other firm attorneys and with the firm through automated marketing and client relationship management systems
    - ❒ Participation in the development of marketing automation systems
- Committee and team marketing participation
    - ❒ Marketing Committee, team marketing pitches, and events
- Marketing mentorship
    - ❒ Helping junior lawyers learn to build referral networks

Creating a more granular breakdown of activities and contributions is easy enough, but these should get you started. We recommend assigning points to each contribution and compensating per point. For example, if points pay $1,000 each and someone earned 5 points, that person would receive $5,000.

Building a brand takes significant work on the part of the partners, and those who contribute to the quality of the firm's brand and name recognition should receive consideration in the compensation system, even though it is often difficult to identify the results of these efforts in the short run.

Compensating for Law Firm Wealth Creation: Systems and Intellectual Property

Contributing to the firm's operational excellence is typically most recognized through compensation for committee service or a specific identifiable task, such as heading up a committee to evaluate the firm's technology. This type of contribution benefits the entire organization, and we usually encounter very little resistance when suggesting awards for specifically identifiable projects. Consideration for these contributions, especially committee service, is often considered in the relevant area or under a broader firm management category.

Beyond this, however, law firms rarely focus on firm-wide practice-level best practices. It is common for practice management systems, or how a universal practice management system is applied, to vary among practices within the same firm. Because of the diffuse power structure in many law firms, partners who control large business books enjoy a high degree of autonomy and often protect their unique systems and processes.

Many want to protect their ultimate ability to move firms, which can create resistance to contributing to the firm's secret sauce. Law firms should transcend this mentality and incentivize partners to contribute to the systems and intellectual property that benefit the whole.

Consider the following KPIs and contribution examples to assist in creating rewards and incentives for contributing to the firm's intellectual wealth stores.

- Contributions to the firm's client relationship management and marketing automation systems (CRM MAS)
  - ❒ Updating client and contact records
- Working within and supporting the development of a firm-wide case management system
  - ❒ Keeping client and case records current
  - ❒ Contributing automated workflows
- Contributing high-quality legal content and repeatable processes to the firm's collective knowledge stores
  - ❒ Contributing to forms, templates, reusable documents (soon part of the AI stores), and policies and procedures
- Creating and following practice and management protocols
  - ❒ Cooperation with risk management protocols

Contributing to the firm's intellectual process stores falls into that category that we call wealth creation, which includes a group of subjective contributions. Compensating for wealth creation is accomplished by balancing the profit allocated to objective and subjective pools. For example, after carefully reviewing its economic needs and strategic goals, a firm allocates 70% of its net income to economic performance and 30% to wealth creation. Firms can modulate these amounts to correlate with their strategic and financial needs. Branding and marketing is a wealth creation factor and would receive a share of the net income allocated to the subjective factors.

Finally, law firms should consider a package of long-term incentives that encourage full participation in the firm's success. Law firms that overcome resistance to investing current-year income into the firm's future have a long-term advantage over their competitors who think short-term.

Compensating for Law Firm Wealth Creation: Cultural Support and Development

What is a team player worth? How important is it to have people think beyond the walls of their practices and contribute to the success of others? Anyone who has worked in the private practice of law will likely encounter someone highly successful economically but toxic to the culture.

Hopefully, you have also had the opportunity to work with someone interested in the success of others and the entire firm. All else being equal, the toxic partner is a weakness for a firm and a detriment to its cultural development. However, the partner who is successful and contributes to the success of others and the quality of the firm's culture should have this behavior reinforced.

Over the past two decades, we have worked with numerous firms and on numerous lateral deals, and the value of a successful collaborative partner in these instances was immeasurable. It is often the factor that makes the difference whether someone joined the firm or not.

Cultural support contributions fall into that category that we call wealth creation, which includes a group of subjective contributions. Compensating for wealth creation is accomplished by balancing the profit allocated to objective and subjective pools. For example, after carefully reviewing its economic needs and strategic goals, a firm allocates 70% of its net income to economic performance and 30% to wealth creation. Firms can modulate these amounts to correlate with their strategic and financial needs. Cultural support contributions are a wealth creation factor and would receive a share of the net income allocated to the subjective factors.

As a starting point, here are examples of KPIs, behaviors, or traits a firm can consider:

- Citizenship
  - Firm first attitude
  - Embracing the firm's mission, vision and values
  - Showing up in public for the firm
- Fairness
  - Consideration of the needs of others
  - Willingness to compromise for the greater good
- Collaboration
  - Able to work well with others
  - Sharing information and support
- Team Orientation
  - Value the contributions of others
  - Contribute to the success of others
- Stewardship
  - Ownership mentality
  - Accountable
  - Responsible
  - Willingness to serve

It is difficult to put an actual score on contributions in these areas, but some structure can apply. Each firm must develop and refine its unique criteria, but start with the basics outlined here. Cultural support is essential to a healthy law firm and sometimes gets lost in economic formulas and spreadsheets.

Compensating for Law Firm Management

It is highly recommended that managing partners or those who make significant management contributions be paid. Objective systems that rely heavily on timekeeper and origination performance measures will need a feature that allocates compensation for non-client-related management contributions.

Subjective and equity ownership-based compensation systems tend to use a rough justice approach to rewarding management contributions. For example, if a managing partner also owns significant equity in the firm, the implied bargain, although not always true, is that they benefit enough from their efforts, and no additional compensation is necessary. Alternatively, someone with fewer points might suffer a detriment and deserve additional compensation.

In most cases, a managing partner does not lose ownership points while managing the firm and, as a result, does not suffer negative impacts from their service.

Firms that use base salaries as part of their compensation scheme tend to consider managing partner or management committee service when setting the base. Finally, many firms do not compensate managing partners, view it as a duty, a coveted position, or simply don't consider management contributions in their compensation formula.

Fully compensating managing partners and committee members is more challenging for small and mid-sized firms that rely on economic contributions from partners who also manage. Which should first come: improved performance followed by incentives or incentives to create improved performance? This question is a standard stumbling block for many firms.

It is best to make this decision using a structured process and design a compensation plan that fairly compensates firm management and leadership. We recommend compensating for significant firm management contributions not covered by one of the other subjective areas. We recommend making these awards identifiable and treated similarly to an operating expense, paid before allocating net income to the partners.

We have experienced firms that pay a set amount annually, compensate for hours worked on management, subjective awards, and some that pay based on revenue. Paying for management affords a measure of accountability to the firm because the time spent managing is not donated.

As a starting point, here are the typical compensated positions and committee service appointments:

- Managing Equity Owner (partner/shareholder/member, etc.)
- Management Committee Members
- Compensation Committee
- Strategic Planning/Long-Range Planning
- Ad Hoc Committees appointed by the Management Committee
- Committees or service positions not covered by other compensation factors—for example, marketing awards consider marketing service

The first step to creating a practical compensation approach for management is to develop roles, responsibilities, and expectations for each compensated position. Next, consider the time requirements for each position and decide on an approach-set amount, hourly reimbursement, subjective award, evaluation-based award, share of revenue, and so on.

Compensation for management benefits everyone and also introduces accountability regarding expectations and cost management.

Law Firm Equity Partner Compensation: Capital and Investing

A constant topic of discussion among law firm equity owners is capital retained by the firm and remuneration for that investment in the firm's operations. Many law firms withhold current-year earnings as a source of working capital; some also use a line of credit as needed.

Relatively few law firms have adequate capital policies or fixed capital contribution requirements. Law firms are overwhelmingly set up as pass-through entities for tax purposes, meaning law firm equity owners pay tax-allocated income to them at the firm level, even if they did not personally receive the actual cash from their firm.

When law firms hold back earnings to operate the firm or to make significant purchases, equity owners effectively pay tax on money they have not personally received. These withheld funds act as financing for the firm to operate and produce greater future profits.

Some firms compensate equity owners for their capital invested in the firm, but in our experience, most don't. We advocate that equity owners receive at least a market interest rate on these invested funds as an incentive to rely less on debt. Two simple approaches to compensating for contributed capital include paying a stated interest rate or allocating a portion of net income. Each owner's capital balance would determine the amount of income earned.

Law firm equity owners might make more sound investments and spending decisions if they invested or used their money (capital) to finance these initiatives. Many law firm equity owners mistakenly believe that an expense or investment did not impact the firm's finances because a line of credit was used to cover the cost. We appreciate the practical conflicts, especially with younger equity owners, but owning a business takes money. Banks can help, but everyone should have some skin in the game.

Wrapping Up

In conclusion, associate and partner compensation in law firms is a nuanced and strategic imperative. It is not merely a matter of paying lawyers what they are worth but also considers market dynamics, firm economics, and the organization's cultural values. By navigating this complex interplay, law firms can create compensation structures that attract and retain top talent while aligning with their broader strategic goals and values.

Here are some critical considerations for law firms when developing their compensation structures:

1. **Market dynamics**: Law firms must consider the prevailing market rates for legal talent in their region or practice area. This element includes the salaries of other lawyers and the evaluation of competitors' bonuses and benefits.
2. **Firm economics**: Law firms must also consider their financial situation when setting compensation rates, including factors such as the firm's profitability, overhead costs, and growth plans.
3. **Cultural values**: The firm's cultural values also affect compensation decisions. For example, a firm that values teamwork and collaboration may emphasize subjective contributions more. In contrast, a firm that values individual achievement may be more likely to have a merit-based formulaic compensation system.

By carefully considering all of these factors, law firms can create compensation structures that are fair to lawyers, competitive in the market, and aligned with the firm's overall goals and values.

Chapter 11
The Role of Technology in the Modern Legal Landscape

Colin S. Levy

In recent years, the legal industry has undergone a significant transformation in its perception and adoption of technology. Once considered a luxury, technology has now become an indispensable tool for law firms and legal departments alike. This shift is evident in the consistent increase in technology spending within the legal sector over the past decade. Law firms frequently leverage technology to automate administrative tasks, boost productivity, and enhance data-driven decision making. Similarly, legal departments have embraced technology to improve efficiency, align with business needs, and increase overall effectiveness.

Budgeting and Return on Investment

The allocation of resources toward technology investments varies among law firms, with the typical range being a small percentage of their total revenue. The American Bar Association's comprehensive Legal Technology Survey Report illuminates a stark dichotomy in technology adoption across the legal profession in 2024. While 65.2% of surveyed firms allocate dedicated resources to technology, the distribution reveals a troubling digital divide: an overwhelming 94.1% of mid-sized firms (50-99 attorneys) embrace technological budgeting, while the majority of solo practitioners (55.4%) operate without any structured technology investment framework.

For firms that have crossed the technological Rubicon by establishing dedicated budgets, the trajectory is decidedly upward—53.7% report increased allocations compared to previous fiscal cycles, while 23.2% maintain consistent investment levels. Industry strategists advocate for technology appropriations between 4-7% of total operational expenditures, with granular recommendations approaching $300 monthly per attorney for software acquisition alone, exclusive of essential training investments.

The survey unmasks the profound influence of experiential feedback on technology procurement decisions, with staff input emerging as the dominant factor (39.2% rate it "very influential"), eclipsing traditional marketing channels—both print and digital advertisements register a mere 0.4% influence rating. This underscores the ascendance of practical utility over promotional messaging in the legal technology marketplace.

Concerning security infrastructure, legal practitioners demonstrate selective adoption patterns: while fundamental protections like spam filtration (77.7%) and software firewalls (72.6%) enjoy widespread implementation, more sophisticated safeguards such as email encryption (41.1%) and comprehensive disk encryption (17%) remain conspicuously underutilized. Perhaps most alarming is the knowledge gap revealed by the 19.9% of respondents unaware of their firm's security policies and the 12.8% who cannot identify which protective mechanisms their organization employs.

The smallest legal enterprises, while allocating proportionally less to technology, are experiencing the most dramatic growth trajectory—solo practitioners' software investments are surging at 56%, more than doubling the industry average. This acceleration coincides with the broad migration toward cloud-based practice management solutions, now utilized by 73% of firms, and heightened cybersecurity consciousness, with 60% implementing formal protective protocols.

Despite these fluctuations, the legal industry has witnessed a steady rise in technology spending over the past decade, recognizing its impact on profitability and efficiency.

Effective technology adoption requires careful budgeting and a clear understanding of the potential return on investment (ROI). Developing a comprehensive technology budget involves assessing current technology infrastructure, identifying gaps and opportunities for improvement, and prioritizing investments based on their expected impact and value. This may require collaboration between legal, IT, and finance departments to ensure that technology spending is aligned with overall business strategy.

To justify technology investments, law firms and legal departments must be able to demonstrate their ROI. This involves measuring the tangible benefits of technology adoption, such as increased efficiency, productivity, and client satisfaction, as well as intangible benefits, such as improved risk management and competitive advantage. Building a strong business case for technology investments requires clearly articulating the expected benefits, costs, and risks, as well as providing concrete metrics and key performance indicators (KPIs) to track progress and measure success.

Client Expectations and Competition

In today's digital age, clients have heightened expectations when it comes to their legal providers' use of technology. They anticipate seamless digital communication, real-time access to information, and secure online collaboration. Law firms that employ client-facing technologies, such as portals and automated updates, have reported higher levels of client satisfaction and retention.

Clients increasingly desire digital access to their legal matters, such as the ability to use dashboards or client portals to access and provide information securely, view the status of their cases, and communicate with their legal team. These tools not only enhance transparency and convenience for clients but also streamline workflows for legal professionals. Organizations that invest in user-friendly, secure client portals can differentiate themselves in the market and strengthen client relationships.

However, it is crucial for law firms and legal departments to address client concerns surrounding privacy and data security when adopting new technologies. Robust cybersecurity measures, regular security audits, and clear communication about data protection practices are essential to maintain client trust and comply with regulatory requirements.

The legal market is facing increasing disruption from alternative legal service providers (ALSPs) and technology companies, which offer innovative, technology-driven solutions. To remain competitive, law firms and legal departments must differentiate themselves by leveraging technology to enhance client service, improve efficiency, and drive profitability.

The rise of ALSPs has created new forms of competition for traditional law firms and legal departments, particularly in areas such as personal injury, contractual negotiations, and immigration. ALSPs offer specialized services at lower rates than law firms, provide opportunities for cost reduction, and efficiently handle large-scale processes involving substantial data sets. While initially focused on low-cost services, ALSPs now attract clients seeking specific legal expertise, with more than half of law firms using ALSPs for this purpose rather than cost savings.

To compete effectively with ALSPs and technology companies, law firms and legal departments must embrace innovation and adopt a client-centric approach. This involves investing in technology solutions that streamline processes, improve communication, and deliver value to clients. Developing niche expertise and providing high-quality, personalized service can help differentiate law firms and legal departments from the commoditized offerings of ALSPs. Furthermore, organizations can explore strategic partnerships and collaborations with ALSPs and technology providers to enhance their capabilities and expand their reach.

Risk Management and Malpractice Prevention

Technology plays a vital role in mitigating errors and enhancing compliance in various aspects of legal practice, including document automation, calendaring, and oversight. Case studies have demonstrated how the absence of proper technology integration has led to malpractice issues, while its effective use has prevented such problems. To minimize risks, best practices involve thoroughly vetting and integrating risk management tools into legal workflows.

It is crucial for lawyers to educate themselves on the benefits and risks of relevant technology, as outlined in the duty of tech competence now in effect for lawyers in the majority of states in the US. This duty requires attorneys to maintain a level of proficiency in the use of technology to effectively represent their clients and protect sensitive information. Failure to do so can result in ethical violations and malpractice claims.

In recent times, the use of generative AI tools, such as ChatGPT, has become a topic of concern in the legal industry. While these tools can assist lawyers in drafting documents and conducting research, they have been known to provide false information on occasion. Several lawyers have faced consequences for relying on ChatGPT to help them draft briefs, as the AI-generated non-existent cases to support their legal positions. This highlights the importance of carefully evaluating the accuracy and reliability of AI-generated content before incorporating it into legal work.

Strategic Planning and Implementation

Developing a successful technology strategy begins with establishing a long-term vision that aligns with the organization's goals and client needs. This process involves creating a technology roadmap, evaluating and selecting appropriate tools, and incorporating flexibility to adapt to new developments. It is essential for law firms and legal departments to ensure that their technology investments support their overall business objectives.

Before evaluating technological solutions, it is crucial to have a systematic strategy in place. This starts with conducting a thorough analysis of existing processes and identifying pain points. Understanding the root causes of these pain points is essential to determine the most effective solutions. Only then should organizations begin to evaluate potential technologies.

When assessing technology solutions, law firms and legal departments must be clear-eyed about their capabilities and understand the extent of change required for implementation. It is also important to consider how the new technology will integrate with the existing set of tools. Involving key stakeholders and end-users in the evaluation process is crucial to ensure that personnel understand and can effectively utilize the solution's features.

As legal technology continues to transform the industry, it is essential for law firms and legal departments to invest time and resources in training their employees to use these tools effectively. However, training can be expensive and challenging to get right, making it a significant hurdle for many organizations.

To ensure that training is effective, many organizations are turning to microlearning—an approach that involves short, focused training sessions lasting a few minutes. These bite-sized lessons allow users to learn at their own pace and can be easily integrated into busy schedules. By breaking down complex topics into specific, manageable pieces of information, microlearning aligns with people's short attention spans and enables them to retain knowledge more effectively.

Microlearning can be delivered through various formats, such as videos, interactive modules, or even gamified content, making it engaging and accessible for learners. This approach also allows for the creation of personalized learning paths, tailoring the training to each individual's needs and roles within the organization.

Law firms and legal departments should also consider implementing a continuous learning culture, where employees are encouraged to develop their skills and knowledge consistently. This can involve regular training sessions, access to online learning resources, and opportunities for peer-to-peer knowledge sharing. By prioritizing ongoing training and adopting innovative approaches like microlearning, organizations can ensure that their staff is well-equipped to leverage technology and drive success.

Practice-Specific Solutions

Technology solutions must be customized to cater to the unique needs of different practice areas, ranging from legal research and document management in litigation to client communication in estate planning. Law firms and legal departments should explore both specialized legal software and general-purpose tools to find the most suitable fit for their specific requirements.

In litigation practice, e-discovery tools can streamline the process of collecting, reviewing, and producing electronic evidence. These platforms offer features such as data processing, predictive coding, and analytics to help legal teams efficiently manage large volumes of data and identify relevant documents.

For legal research and document review, AI-powered tools can assist attorneys in finding relevant case law, statutes, and secondary sources. These platforms leverage natural language processing and machine learning to provide more accurate and efficient search results, saving time and improving the quality of legal research. Additionally, comprehensive case law research and analytics tools enable attorneys to gain valuable insights and make data-driven decisions.

In contract management, solutions can automate the creation, execution, and storage of legal agreements. These tools offer features such as templating, e-signature, version control, and AI-assisted contract drafting, review, and negotiation. By leveraging these platforms, organizations can reduce the time and effort required to manage contracts while improving accuracy and compliance.

For intellectual property practices, tools can help manage patent and trademark portfolios, automate filings, and monitor deadlines. These platforms provide features such as docketing, renewal reminders, and collaboration tools to help IP attorneys stay organized and efficient.

By carefully selecting and implementing practice-specific technology solutions, law firms and legal departments can enhance their service delivery, improve efficiency, and gain a competitive edge in their respective areas of expertise.

Remote Work and Data Security

The COVID-19 pandemic has accelerated the adoption of remote work practices in the legal industry, forcing law firms and legal departments to rapidly adapt to a new reality. This sudden shift has highlighted the critical role of technology in enabling seamless collaboration, communication, and productivity in a remote work environment.

Organizations have had to swiftly implement remote work tools, such as video conferencing platforms, secure file sharing systems, and cloud-based practice management software. These tools have allowed legal professionals to continue serving clients, attending virtual court proceedings, and collaborating with colleagues despite physical distancing requirements.

However, the transition to remote work has not been without challenges. Law firms and legal departments have had to address concerns surrounding data privacy, security, and confidentiality when accessing sensitive information remotely. Ensuring that all team members have access to reliable technology infrastructure and providing adequate training on new tools has also been a significant undertaking.

Despite these challenges, the shift to remote work has also presented opportunities for law firms and legal departments to reassess their technology strategies and accelerate digital transformation initiatives. The pandemic has highlighted the need for resilient, agile, and scalable technology solutions that can support the evolving needs of the legal industry.

As law firms and legal departments increasingly rely on technology to store, process, and transmit sensitive client information, data privacy and security have become paramount concerns. Legal professionals have a duty to protect client confidentiality and maintain the integrity of their data, and failure to do so can result in significant legal and reputational consequences.

To address these concerns, organizations must implement robust data privacy and security measures. This includes ensuring compliance with relevant regulations, such as the General Data Protection Regulation (GDPR) in the European Union and the California Consumer Privacy Act (CCPA) in the United States.

Best practices for safeguarding client information include implementing strong access controls, encrypting sensitive data both in transit and at rest, regularly monitoring systems for potential breaches, and providing comprehensive staff training on data privacy and security protocols.

Law firms and legal departments should also conduct thorough due diligence when selecting technology vendors and ensure that their solutions meet stringent security standards. Contractual agreements with vendors should include provisions addressing data ownership, confidentiality, and incident response procedures.

Emerging Technologies

The legal industry is witnessing the rise of various emerging technologies that have the potential to transform the way legal services are delivered. These technologies include blockchain, smart contracts, and artificial intelligence (AI).

Blockchain technology offers a secure and transparent way to record transactions in the legal context. It provides a more reliable and tamper-evident method for handling records, evidence, property rights, and the notarization of documents. For lawyers, blockchain offers a robust platform for managing transactions that require a high degree of trust and verification without the need for a central authority. This has significant implications for areas like real estate transactions, intellectual property rights management, and maintaining chain-of-custody for evidence.

In the real estate industry, blockchain-based platforms like Propy and Ubitquity are being used to streamline property transactions by enabling the secure and efficient transfer of ownership, recording of land titles, and processing of payments through smart contracts. These platforms reduce the need for intermediaries, lower costs, and increase transparency in the property buying and selling process.

Blockchain technology is also being used to create immutable records of intellectual property assets, such as patents, trademarks, and copyrights. Platforms like IPwe and Bernstein use blockchain to securely store IP-related data, track ownership changes, and facilitate licensing transactions through smart contracts. This helps to prevent fraud, simplify IP management, and enable faster and more efficient monetization of IP assets.

Smart contracts, self-executing contracts with the terms directly written into code, operate on the blockchain and carry immense potential for the legal industry. They automate contractual obligations, reducing the need for intermediaries and thus the time and cost associated with contract execution. For lawyers, this means a shift from drafting static documents to creating dynamic, self-enforcing contracts that can automatically respond to certain triggers.

In supply chain management, smart contracts on blockchain platforms are being used to automate and streamline processes. For example, in the food industry, IBM Food Trust uses blockchain to improve food traceability, enable more efficient recalls, and facilitate secure information sharing among supply chain participants. Smart contracts can automatically execute payments and update inventory records when predefined conditions are met, such as the completion of a delivery.

Insurance claims processing is another area where blockchain-based smart contracts are being explored to automate and expedite the process. Etherisc, for instance, has developed a decentralized flight insurance application that uses smart contracts to automatically issue policies and process claims based on flight data. If a flight is delayed or canceled, the smart contract triggers a payout to the policyholder without requiring manual intervention from the insurer.

Legal agreement platforms like OpenLaw and Clause are enabling the creation of self-executing contracts using smart contract technology. These platforms allow lawyers to draft, negotiate, and execute contracts that automatically enforce the agreed-upon terms and conditions. For example, a smart contract could automatically release funds from escrow to a contractor upon completion of a project milestone, as verified by IoT sensors or other data sources.

The legal industry is witnessing the rise of various emerging technologies that have the potential to transform the way legal services are delivered. Among these, generative AI, particularly Large Language Models (LLMs), is creating significant impact across multiple aspects of legal practice.

Large Language Models (LLMs) are at the forefront of generative AI, particularly in their application within the legal sector. As AI systems that have been trained on vast corpora of text, LLMs are adept at generating human-like text, which is especially useful in the language-heavy field of law. The use of LLMs can significantly enhance the efficiency and quality of legal services in various ways, including contract drafting and analysis, legal research, due diligence processes, and client communication.

In contract drafting and analysis, LLMs like GPT-4 and Claude are being deployed by law firms to automate the creation of initial contract drafts, identify potential issues in existing contracts, and suggest alternative clauses that better protect client interests. Tools such as CoCounsel by Casetext and Harvey AI assist attorneys in quickly generating contract templates that can be customized to specific client needs, reducing drafting time from hours to minutes while maintaining quality and compliance with relevant regulations.

For legal research, platforms like Vlex's Vincent and Lexis+ AI use LLMs to help attorneys quickly find relevant case law, statutes, and legal opinions. These tools can analyze vast legal databases and provide precise answers to complex legal questions, summarize lengthy court decisions, and identify relevant precedents that might otherwise be overlooked in traditional research methods. This capability allows lawyers to provide more comprehensive advice to clients in significantly less time.

In due diligence processes, LLMs are transforming how law firms review large volumes of documents during mergers and acquisitions, real estate transactions, and compliance audits. Solutions like Kira Systems and Luminance employ AI to automatically extract and categorize key information from thousands of documents, flagging potential risks and anomalies that require attorney attention. This technology reduces the review time by up to 90% while improving accuracy and allowing legal professionals to focus on higher-value analytical tasks.

Client communication is another area benefiting from generative AI, with law firms implementing AI-powered chatbots and virtual assistants to handle routine client inquiries, schedule appointments, and provide basic legal information. These tools ensure clients receive immediate responses outside of business hours and free up attorneys' time for more complex matters. Some firms are also using LLMs to generate personalized client updates and explanations of complex legal concepts in plain language, enhancing client satisfaction and understanding.

Despite their benefits, it is imperative to understand the limitations and ethical considerations of employing LLMs. Lawyers must use these technologies responsibly, ensuring they do not rely blindly on the outputs without applying their professional judgment. They must remain vigilant about maintaining client confidentiality and upholding the profession's ethical standards. Bar associations across multiple jurisdictions are developing specific guidelines for AI use in legal practice, emphasizing the need for human oversight, transparency with clients about AI use, and verification of AI-generated content before submission to courts or opposing counsel.

While these examples demonstrate the transformative potential of generative AI in the legal industry, it is important to note that the adoption of these technologies is still evolving. As legal regulatory frameworks adapt to accommodate these new technologies and as more legal professionals become comfortable with their use, we can expect to see increasingly sophisticated applications that fundamentally reshape how legal services are delivered to clients.

Access to Justice and Ethical Considerations

Technology has the potential to play a significant role in improving access to justice for underserved communities. By leveraging digital tools, legal services can be made more affordable, accessible, and efficient.

Online dispute resolution (ODR) platforms, for example, can provide a cost-effective and convenient way for individuals to resolve legal disputes without the need for expensive court proceedings. These platforms use technology to facilitate negotiation, mediation, and arbitration processes, making justice more accessible to a wider range of people.

Legal chatbots and self-help tools can also assist individuals in understanding their legal rights and navigating complex legal processes. These tools can provide personalized guidance, generate legal documents, and connect individuals with relevant resources and support services.

Law firms and legal departments can contribute to improving access to justice by supporting and collaborating with initiatives that leverage technology to provide legal assistance to underserved communities. This can include partnering with legal aid organizations, providing pro bono services, and investing in the development of innovative legal tech solutions.

As the legal industry becomes increasingly reliant on technology, it is crucial to consider the ethical implications of its use. Lawyers have a professional responsibility to maintain competence in the use of technology and to ensure that its use does not compromise their ethical duties to clients.

The duty of technology competence, which has been recognized in the majority of US states, requires lawyers to keep abreast of changes in technology and its potential impact on their practice. This includes understanding the benefits and risks of using specific tools and platforms and being able to use them effectively to serve clients.

The use of AI in legal decision making raises ethical concerns. Lawyers must be able to explain and justify the basis for their decisions, which may be challenging when relying on opaque AI algorithms. There is also a risk that AI systems may perpetuate biases or make errors that could have serious consequences for clients.

To address these ethical considerations, the legal industry must develop clear guidelines and best practices for the responsible use of technology. This may include establishing standards for transparency, accountability, and fairness in the development and deployment of legal tech tools.

Concluding Thoughts

The role of technology in the modern legal landscape is undeniably crucial. As the industry continues to evolve, law firms and legal departments that proactively embrace innovation and adopt a strategic approach to technology will be best positioned to succeed in an increasingly competitive market. By investing in the right tools, fostering a culture of continuous learning, and prioritizing the ethical and responsible use of technology, legal professionals can unlock new opportunities, enhance their service offerings, and ultimately better serve their clients in the digital age.

Key lessons to take with you are:

1. Technology is no longer a luxury but an essential tool for law firms and legal departments to improve efficiency, productivity, and client service. Effective technology adoption requires careful budgeting, clear ROI metrics, and alignment with overall business objectives.
2. Client expectations and competition from alternative legal service providers are driving the need for technology adoption in the legal industry.
3. Successful technology implementation depends on strategic planning, thorough evaluation of solutions, and effective change management.
4. Emerging technologies like blockchain, smart contracts, and AI have the potential to transform legal services delivery, but their adoption requires a clear understanding of their capabilities and limitations.
5. Technology can play a significant role in improving access to justice for underserved communities, but its use must be guided by ethical considerations and professional responsibility.

As the legal landscape continues to evolve, it is imperative for lawyers and legal professionals to embrace technology and adapt to the changing environment. This requires a proactive approach to learning about and implementing new tools and solutions, as well as a willingness to challenge traditional ways of working and thinking.

I call upon all legal professionals to act by:

1. Educating themselves about the latest technological advancements and their potential applications in legal practice.
2. Collaborating with IT professionals, legal technologists, and other experts to develop and implement effective technology strategies.
3. Investing in training and professional development to build the skills and knowledge needed to leverage technology effectively.
4. Prioritizing data privacy and security in all technology initiatives and ensuring compliance with relevant regulations and ethical standards.
5. Exploring opportunities to use technology to improve access to justice and make legal services more affordable and accessible to underserved communities.

By embracing these actions and committing to ongoing innovation and adaptation, the legal industry can harness the power of technology to drive success, better serve clients, and shape the future of legal services in the digital age.

Chapter 12

Cybersecurity and Data Privacy for Law Firms

Getting Started

Eric B. Levine[12]

One of the many challenges facing law firms in this digital age is protecting data from unwanted disclosure by outside threat actors. Law firm leadership is faced with the daunting task of not only understanding the concepts of cybersecurity and data privacy, but of taking steps to recognize threats that accompany the possession of confidential business and client information, implementing safeguards to protect and monitor such information, responding to threats to the sanctity of such information, and dealing with the ramifications of an intrusion and exploitation of business and client information. Cybersecurity is an issue that is here to stay, and a law firm's success can be affected greatly, either positively or negatively, based on the firm's approach to protecting its critical data.

The challenges of cybersecurity and data privacy are monumental, and unfortunately, many law firms find themselves lacking the necessary tools to meet the challenges. Resources addressing same are numerous, and it is easy to get overwhelmed by the magnitude of addressing the issue without guidance. This chapter is designed to help a law firm get started on addressing cybersecurity and data privacy. It will address the concepts of cybersecurity, identify the risks law firms face, how to start development

[12] The author would like to thank Gozde Celik, Esq. of Lindabury McCormick Estabrook & Cooper, P.C., for her invaluable assistance with this chapter.

of a cybersecurity policy, securing client information and data, and the legal and ethical landscape. It is not intended to capture all of the nuance of cybersecurity and data privacy, but rather to assist law firm leadership in beginning to identify critical issues and developing conceptual tools to assist in responding to those issues.[13]

Moreover, as cybersecurity and data privacy are governed in large part by state law and in certain instances international law, this chapter addresses cybersecurity and data privacy on a general level. Readers are advised to research the applicable law in their respective jurisdictions and seek the advice of experienced cybersecurity practitioners. Readers should be mindful that there is momentum to enact federal legislation in the United States on data privacy, but as of the drafting of this article, no single comprehensive piece of legislation has been enacted.

Cybersecurity for Law Firms

The terms "cybersecurity" and "data privacy" are critical concepts for law firms to understand as they are intertwined with the fabric of the legal community. They are two distinct terms, and while they inevitably overlap in practice, it is critical to understand the differences between them. "Cybersecurity" can be described as the application of technologies, controls, and processes in an effort to safeguard computer systems, networks, programs, devices, and data from unauthorized access by third party threat actors. Put another way, cybersecurity encompasses the technological aspects or tools used for protecting a law firm's client data and the firm's own business information. "Data Privacy" is a broader concept and deals with the protection of personal data from individuals or entities that should not have access to such data. In addition to protecting data, Data Privacy also encompasses the ability of individuals to decide how their information is used, who can access their personal information, and how that information should be used.

Law firms are attractive targets for threat actors seeking to obtain confidential information for unlawful uses as the practice of law requires that lawyers come into possession and utilize confidential client information in almost all facets of a law firm's business model. Whether it be in a family law context, assisting with tax and estate planning, evaluating corporate

[13] ABA TechReport 2022, December 29, 2022, Cybersecurity for Law Firms: What Legal Professionals Should Know.

data related to mergers, acquisitions and divestiture, analyzing labor and employment issues, intellectual property issues, or developing litigation strategies, law firms require information from their clients that necessarily include confidential information (such as social security numbers, addresses, family composition, travel information, medical records, and financial/asset information) and sensitive business data (such as revenues, proprietary technical data, client lists, and employee data). The data a law firm possesses can present a threat actor with the tools needed to accomplish identity theft, divert funds, provide a basis for extortionist tactics against law firms lest its information be leaked onto the dark web, or even just be locked by a threat actor so a law firm cannot access it without paying a ransom.

Moreover, law firms vary in size, sophistication, and financial resources, each of which impact a firm's ability to maintain a robust data privacy defense. While larger, more mature firms may have ample cybersecurity budgets dedicated security staff, and possess a sophisticated understanding of data security, small or mid-size firms may not be similarly situated, leaving them more vulnerable to attacks. Law firms are also confronted with ever increasing client demands for instantaneous responses which warrant reliance on technology, as well as being confronted with the dynamic nature of evolving technology that creates a knowledge gap between attorneys who are up to date on such changes, which tend to be younger members of a law firm, and those who are not up to date, which can include more senior, less technically savvy attorneys. Moving fast and not fully understanding the threats associated with technology creates an opportunity for disaster. The idea behind establishing comprehensive cybersecurity and data privacy measures is to create layers of controls to protect a firm's data, including infrastructure (hardware and software), a dedicated team, constant staff training, and utilizing insurance products. The more layers a firm has, and the more sophisticated each layer is, the harder it is for a threat actor to pierce the layers and gain access to data.

Identifying Risks

The first step any law firm must take in protecting its data is to acknowledge that protecting data must become an enterprise concern, meaning it must be contemplated by the firm leadership as part of an everyday business practice. The implications of data privacy and cybersecurity should be considered when making purchasing decisions, employment decisions, hiring decisions, and as part of practice group development. If a law firm is not expressly including cybersecurity and data privacy in its on-going operations, the chances that such a firm will suffer a loss of data and accompanying loss of clients, revenue, and reputation harm are increased. This means that understanding the risks that law firms face must be an integral part of establishing a firm culture of good data security hygiene.

Types of Risks

The following are a sample of types of risks that law firms face related to data privacy:

1. **Ransomware attacks**: Ransomware attacks are when third party threat actors use malware to harm, disrupt, or gain unauthorized access to a computer system. By encrypting or locking a law firm's files once access is gained and demanding a ransom payment (usually in bitcoin) for the decryption key, threat actors hold organizations hostage until they make a payment. While at times payment of the ransom seems like the easiest way to quickly regain access to files and a return to business, payment of a ransom is a complicated response with several ramifications and is not a guarantee of data restoration of continued privacy. A firm victimized by a ransomware attack should immediately consult with its insurance carrier, local and federal law enforcement, and experienced cybersecurity counsel without delay.
2. **Insider threats**: The threat of data theft or information leak can sometimes originate inside a firm, such as from a disgruntled employee or even a former employee who still has access to a firm's computer network. Such insider threats are hard to guard against, especially in larger firms with multiple offices, but firm leadership can take certain steps to reduce the risk, such as restricting access to information only to those persons who require it to perform their job functions. This is what is known as the Principle of Least Privilege, meaning that each employee has access to the least amount of information they need to properly perform their job. Files can be segregated, password protected, and even encrypted, leaving it available only to those that "need to know."
3. **Fraudulent wire transfer/transactional risk**: Wire transfers are a popular method for threat actors and can present several risks to law firms which tend utilize the process frequently. The risk primarily revolve around fraud, potential for scams, and irreversible

transactions. Threat actors frequently use wire transfers as a method of payment in fraudulent schemes, and once money is transferred, it is difficult or impossible to recover.

4. **Social engineering schemes**: Social engineering is the manipulation of people into performing acts or divulging information using psychological tactics such as when a threat actor poses as a friend seeking assistance or touting a good/service in order to induce a response, like clicking on a link or opening an embedded file which is normally a host for malware. Social engineering exploits human characteristics, like curiosity and the desire to help a friend, to prompt a response and is one of the more common cybersecurity threats law firms encounter.
5. **Phishing/Email/text threats**: This is the practice of sending emails or text messages which appear to be from reputable companies or reliable sources in order to induce someone to divulge personal information, such as passwords and credit card numbers or bank information. This is another popular threat actor tool.
6. **Business Email Compromises (BEC)**: A BEC is a type of phishing attack targeting business enterprises. A BEC tries to takes advantage of the seemingly legitimate email address of a person within a company to trick the recipient within the same company into taking a certain action. This is done using high-pressure messages allegedly from a trusted colleague, like an email from a managing partner to a junior associate asking the junior associate to perform a task or send money to the alleged managing partner. BEC attacks differ from other types of email-based attacks on a couple of key areas: They do not contain malware, malicious links, or email attachments, and they target specific individuals within organizations. They are personalized to the intended victim and often are the result of advanced research of the organization by the threat actor.

Developing a Plan

Before a firm begins to assess data privacy risks, it should develop a plan to address data privacy and establish its goals and objectives at the enterprise level. The exercise of drafting a plan helps to enable a firm to understand the need to dedicate the resources and allocate manpower to fulfill the plan, even if it means the hiring of security specialists for assistance. A good place to find resources on how to develop a plan can be found at the website of the National Institute of Standards and Technology

(NIST).[14] NIST provides free guidance on how to implement a framework to address cybersecurity and data privacy. The site also maintains a variety of resources that can help a firm develop a meaningful cybersecurity program. NIST is recognized as a leading authority on cybersecurity and data protection.

Whether you decide to follow the NIST framework or not, a firm's cybersecurity and data privacy plan should include: (1) identifying the scope and location of the firm's data (what do you have and where is it stored?); (2) determining how the firm plans to categorize, store, maintain, and dispose of data; (3) describing steps to be taken to train staff on proper data hygiene and strengthen the firm's data infrastructure using a combination of hardware, software, and even outsourcing functions to third party vendors; (4) delineating how the firm will respond to client concerns and data subject access requests (such as client demands to delete client data from a firm's network); (5) defining how to respond to data incidences/breaches and mitigate related damages; (6) procuring cyber-insurance; (7) developing a process to ensure regulatory compliance; and (8) creating a budget taking into account insurance costs, vendor costs, and equipment procurement. The plan should be written and revisited annually, and be treated like a dynamic document that changes and evolves to match a firm's evolution.

Create a Team

Once a firm has developed its overall data privacy plan, its leadership should establish a formal cybersecurity/data privacy committee and appoint a director or chair of that committee to serve as the firm's information security officer. The committee is vital to a firm's success and appointment thereto should be taken seriously. It is a firm's designated watchdog of vital information and must be manned with proactive individuals tasked with (1) becoming knowledgeable about cybersecurity practices and theory; (2) assessing security risks within the firm; (3) developing cybersecurity and data privacy policies and procedures tailored to the firm's needs; (4) providing periodic reports to firm leadership; (5) creating and revising an annual cybersecurity budget; (6) recommending and overseeing implementation of employee training programs and safety data measures; and (7) monitoring developments in the law and technology.

[14] https://www.nist.gov/cyberframework

The composition of the committee should include a cross-section of attorneys (shareholders/partners and associates) as well as director-level, non-attorney staff and at least one member of the firm's Information Technology (IT) department. It should meet frequently and maintain records of meetings and efforts taken. Note that while it is crucial for a firm's IT department to be part of the committee, a director of IT and an information security officer perform distinct functions. An IT director may have some overlapping duties with an information security officer, but the information security officer's role is more specialized, focusing on maintaining the integrity of the firm's data, while the IT director is concerned with all of the firm's overall technological needs, including hardware and software required to operate a law practice. It is good practice to fill these two roles with different individuals.

Assessing Vulnerabilities and Risk

Once the cybersecurity and data privacy team is in place and a plan is developed, a firm should then identify vulnerabilities in its data infrastructure that could lead to unwanted exposure of data. Understand that no computer system is entirely impregnable so it is almost a certainty that any assessment performed will identify at least one vulnerability. Firms must assess the state of the firm's recordkeeping infrastructure (digital and physical), evaluate physical controls of data, and judge the level of competence of the human component, from firm leadership to support staff. A diligent law firm should perform risk evaluations annually as doing so will help the firm identify areas of weakness and develop remedial measures as its practice. As the state of technology serving law firms and data threats continue to evolve, so must a firm's data privacy efforts. Recognize that obsolescence is a problem that is ever-present; what was a sufficient computer security measure yesterday may be insufficient tomorrow.

Furthermore, risk evaluation and prevention is also a necessary element of obtaining cyber-insurance coverage and fulfilling a law firm's ethical obligations to its client. It may even be implicated if a firm bids for governmental work as many federal, state, and local governments include verification of certain data practices as a pre-condition to any requests for proposal or bid for services. If a firm has weak data privacy practices even if it has never suffered a breach, it could lose work or be denied insurance if viewed as a high risk for data loss.

It is preferable for risk assessments to be performed by a firm's data security committee with the assistance of third party vendors. Records of the results of the assessment should be maintained, as well as documentation of the efforts taken to fortify any vulnerability uncovered. Firms that maintain paper records should assess their physical controls, such as confirming the use of locked file cabinets, video surveillance, restricted entry to sensitive areas of office like records rooms, noting how paper files are accessed and inventoried, and where they are stored. For physical files, an overriding question to ask during an evaluation is whether anyone can walk through an office and take a file without being noticed, and if that occurred, how would it be uncovered?

For digital files, network mapping should be one step in the process. Network mapping is the practice of identifying physical and virtual networks to provide in-depth visibility into a firm's IT infrastructure. It should include identifying what data is stored in what portion of a network, such as a server, and how those servers are connected and accessed. This lets a firm identify where its critical data is located and see how someone can access it. Preparing a data map is also increasingly a requirement of insurance companies and large institutional clients such as financial institutions, as these types of entities want to assess the risk of access to their data that is maintained in a firm's IT infrastructure.

Other areas that must be evaluated for risk of data loss include the use of firm-issued devices like cell phones, laptops and tablets, the level of safety measures provided by a firm's cloud computing provider, the state of the firm's encryption programs and firewalls, the regularity and possible automation of program updates and patching, securing a firm's WIFI system, employee password management, the existence of (or more likely the lack of) endpoint detection and response (EDR) tools, and network monitoring programs. With the advent and pervasiveness of remote working, it is also crucial that a firm purchase and install device tracking software with remote drive/data wiping capabilities. Remote data wiping capabilities are security features that allow a firm to send a command that remotely deletes data from a computing device. Such a command would be issued if a firm laptop or tablet has been lost or stolen, so that the data will not be compromised or extracted from the lost device.

Finally, an indispensable part of a firm's risk assessment includes engaging periodic penetration testing, also known as pen testing, which is a security exercise using a cybersecurity expert that attempts to find and exploit weaknesses in a computer system. It is a simulated cyber-attack aiming to identify any weak spots in a system's defenses. The professional hired will probe a firm's defenses, locate weaknesses, and ultimately issue findings with recommendation on corrective measures.

Utilizing Privilege during Assessments

When performing a vulnerability assessment, it is crucial that a firm involve outside legal counsel experienced in cybersecurity to oversee the assessment in order to shield the results with attorney-client privilege. The scope of privilege differs by jurisdiction, so on this topic, it is especially critical to consult an experienced cyber attorney to ensure that the steps described herein will protect a firm in a specific jurisdiction. The loss of privilege over the results of a vulnerability assessment can have a catastrophic impact on a firm and should not be taken lightly.

In virtually every penetration test and vulnerability assessment, weaknesses will be uncovered and reported. It is common that it will take time to correct any weaknesses, whether due to budgetary concerns, the sheer magnitude of vulnerabilities uncovered, or some other reason such as basic scheduling. Should a firm suffer a cyberbreach before vulnerabilities can be addressed and should a breach be effectuated through an identified vulnerability, the firm suffering the breach is now in possession of a document identifying the very weakness that was exploited. That means that the firm has evidence of a breach of duty of care (the proper maintenance of a computer network) and has arguably breached that duty by not fixing a problem of which the firm was aware. If a client affected by the breach sues the firm for negligence or some other cause of action and seeks disclosure of that report, it would most likely be produced to the plaintiff and would undoubtedly appear at trial as a very powerful plaintiff's exhibit. It is easy to see how such a document, which once was meant to be the guidepost for the firm's proper cybersecurity efforts, is now a literal smoking gun for the plaintiff.

That is why privilege is so important. To avoid the smoking gun scenario, firms should hire outside counsel to manage the vulnerability assessment, thereby allowing the results of those efforts to be subject to attorney-client privilege. A common counter to the assertion of privilege is that the assessment is being performed in the ordinary course of the firm's business and not in anticipation of potential litigation, rendering it a business process and not an action taken in anticipation of litigation. Countering this position requires upfront coordination with outside counsel and an understanding of whether privilege will apply in this context. That coordination should encompass the methods of transmitting information between the vendor performing the vulnerability assessment, outside counsel, and the firm. It should even delineate how retainers are explicitly worded, and how the transmittal of the information is accomplished.

The Human Factor: The Weakest Link

Perhaps the most important element of a firm's on-going effort to protect data is the human factor, meaning the firm's employees. A firm can strengthen technical elements of its defenses, and even automate them, with some degree of assurance that so long as they keep the technical infrastructure up to date and install patches issued by manufacturers and programmers, the technical infrastructure can be counted on to give a consistent level of security. Not so for a firm's employees who are constantly barraged with fake emails and text messages, fraudulent audio and video messages generated by artificial intelligence, and even physical theft of personal devices. People are the targets of choice of threat actors who pry data loose through social engineering, pressure tactics, and reliance on the fatigue people suffer from an endless bombardment of data, rapidly evolving technology, client expectations, deadlines, and the overall stress of the work place environment.

The primary method of preparing staff, from the most senior partner to the newest hired employee, to avoid the myriad threats they face is through constant training. Firm leadership must invest in developing a plan for on-going training of its employees and dedicate an annual budget for that training covering, at a minimum: (1) email security training (spotting false emails/scams/phishing attempts and understanding how to respond to same); (2) internet security training (what is acceptable internet usage while using firm-issued electronic devices); (3), social engineering training (alerting staff about common social engineering tactics, and providing them with the tools to recognize threats and avoid them); (4) acceptable document/information sharing procedures (training staff on secure methods of data transfer such as encrypted files, the use of password protected files, and document sharing programs); and (5) unauthorized software training (instructing staff on who is authorized to install programs onto firm-hosted networks).

Training staff not only reduces the risk of suffering data exposure, but it can assist a firm in qualifying for cyber-insurance and maintaining insurance policies that are issued Most applications of cyber-insurance coverage will ask about prior breaches, infrastructure, but also about the level of employee training. If a firm responds that they have no training in place, they are subject to lower limits, narrower coverage, and even outright rejection of their application. If a firm is able to obtain insurance coverage, some cyber-insurance companies will offer training as part of their services. Firm-wide attendance at training sessions should be mandatory, and written records of attendance should be maintained to provide to insurance carriers if requested.

For some firms, this training can be accomplished with in-house staff, but it can be beneficial to use outside vendors. Attendance records of each training session should be maintained and attendance must be mandatory. It may be necessary for employees to be reminded that failure to attend mandated training could be grounds for discipline, up to and including termination. This may seem draconian, but when one considers the potential ramifications of a breach or successful ransomware attack, it underscores the critical need for all employees to be trained and be constantly vigilant. The downside risk of an employee clicking on an embedded link in an email from a threat actor is just too great and can be an existential threat for some firms.

To create guardrails for staff to follow, a firm should develop written policies governing acceptable usage of firm equipment, remote working, the use of staff's use of personal devices, also known as a Bring Yor Own Device policy (BYOD), social media, emails, and an incident response policy. Each policy should be reviewed by an experienced cyber attorney before this is circulated to each and every employee. The policies should be discussed during training, allowing employees to ask questions to ensure thorough understanding of the policies obligations and purposes. These policies should be centrally maintained and regularly updated.

Obligations of a Firm to Safeguard Data

It is important for a law firm to acknowledge that in addition to good practice and in furtherance of effective cyber-hygiene, there are obligations imposed upon attorneys related to data privacy arising from multiple sources. Those sources include ethical rules, legislation, clients' mandates, and insurance policies. When developing a firm's cybersecurity program, each source must be consulted, complied with, and periodically revisited. Ethically, law firms are governed by rules of professional conduct specific to their jurisdictions, but most jurisdictions have established ethical rules governing attorney competence, supervision of subordinated, protection of client information, and responding to data breaches. For example, the American Bar Association has issued several formal opinions on cyber-related topics that should be reviewed as part of the development of a firm's privacy program.[15]

[15] See, e.g., ABA Formal Opinion 483 "Lawyer's Obligation After an Electronic Data Breach or Cyberattack"; ABA Formal Opinion 495, "Lawyers Working Remotely"; ABA Formal Opinion 498, "Virtual Practice").

From a legislative standpoint, while no single comprehensive federal privacy law is yet enacted, many states have enacted or are in the process of enacting data privacy laws and each firm must evaluate the laws in its specific jurisdiction as part of its data privacy plan. Special care needs to be taken by firms with clients in different states, and even in other countries as a law firm may be subject to a state law of a state or potentially multiple states wherein firm clients are located other than the actual physical location of the firm itself. With the advent of the internet, it is common for firms to have a nationwide client base, the ramifications of which a firm may not realize until a data breach occurs. Certain states with comprehensive data privacy laws such as California, Colorado, Connecticut, Utah, and Virginia may have more stringent privacy laws, including responding to a data breach which is extremely time sensitive. This means such a more stringent data breach response law could exist in the state where the firm's client is located than the law that exists in the state in which a firm is located. It can be jarring to a firm suffering a data breach to find out that despite being based in New Jersey, it must comply with California's breach notification timeline which is dramatically different from New Jersey's. The matter is even more complex if a law firm serves clients in the European Union and is subject to the General Data Privacy Regulation (GDPR). An analysis of the GDPR is beyond the scope of this chapter, but firms servicing international clients are advised to consult with an expert on the GDPR as it is technical, comprehensive, markedly different than most state laws in the United States, and the penalties for non-compliance would be devastating.

Client privacy mandates are important as more clients are requiring law firms to prove the adequacy of their data privacy systems as a condition to being engaged. This is especially true of clients that are themselves subject to legislation on data privacy like health care professionals (subject to HIPAA, also known as the Health Insurance Portability and Accountability Act of 1996, Public Law 104-191) and financial institutions (subject to the Graham-Leach-Bliley Act, also known as the Financial Services Modernization Act of 1999, 15 U.S.C.§§6801-6809 and 15 U.S.C. §§6821-6827). Those clients who are subject to specific laws may be required by those laws to ensure their business associates, like the law firms they utilize, exercise the same level of care that they must. It is not unusual these days for an institutional client to make a condition of engagement that they reserve the right to randomly audit the privacy security measures of law firms servicing them.

Finally, the terms of most cyber-insurance policies will mandate that certain steps are taken by its insureds as preconditions to insurance coverage. These conditions can be as rudimentary as using lock-enabled file cabinets to mandating specific levels of encryption and mandating employee training.

Conclusion

The topics addressed herein constitute the beginning of a long process, the nature of which fills volumes. Beginning to understand the breadth and depth of cybersecurity and data privacy allows firms to move onto the next steps of the process with a sense of confidence that comes from understanding the threats confronting each and every law firm. Do not be fearful if this chapter presented new scenarios or if the prospect of cybersecurity and data privacy seems overwhelming. With the proper planning, commitment by leadership, and prudent use of resources, law firms of any size can take steps to limit their exposure and enhance their defenses, which ultimately protects a firm's clients and adds to financial success.

Chapter 13
Law Firm Succession Planning

Sandra J. Boyer

What happens when an electric vehicle (EV) runs out of charge? It puts itself in park. It will not go anywhere until roadside assistance comes to tow it away. Law firms who—consciously or not—avoid spending time on effective succession planning face the same fate as drivers who are too impatient to fully charge their EVs before hitting the road. They fall short of their destination with no tools to keep going. They put themselves in park.

Law firm succession planning is challenging, it takes more time than anyone would like it to, drains firm energy, and the process can leave you feeling like you are driving around in circles. So, why do it? Simple. To prevent your firm from putting itself in park, being lapped by your competitors, and being towed away before reaching your goal. An effective plan—one that is flexible, addresses special circumstances, values culture, and ebbs and flows with different economic environments—can reinvigorate your firm. It can supply the kinetic energy necessary for the firm not only to endure, but to excel.

The early 2020s pushed the legal industry through a labyrinth of dynamic changes that have made it overwhelming for small to mid-sized law firms to consider dedicating time to focus on succession planning. With so many emergencies to address and fires to put out, how can we pause to discuss what seems like the distant future? Reestablishing succession planning not as a singular effort, but as a component of an overall long-term strategic success strategy may create both the relevancy and the buy-in the firm needs to get the planning up and running. A larger plan may consider thought-provoking interrogatives like:

- Who is driving the private law firm model? Our generation or the next?
- What motivates Millennials and Gen Zs to stay? To work toward ownership?
- Where will the private law firm model be in the next three to five years?
- How and when will artificial intelligence (AI) change roles in firms? In the profession?
- How would we change the focus of our marketing efforts?
- How will operations and client service evolve with tech advances?

Traditionally, we have associated visioning with strategic planning; however, it may also be a key to effective succession planning. Visioning involves acknowledging firm history as it informs current culture, understanding the status quo, and then imagining what we want future firm culture to look like. Firms must draft a blueprint that illustrates what the future firm looks like and how to construct it. From this, the firm can develop a workable, flexible, yet focused succession program.

In this chapter, we will pose thought-provoking questions to help firms draw out overlooked or unconscious biases about succession planning, provide concrete approaches and strategies to jumpstart the process, and introduce ideas you can integrate into your planning. The first step? Understanding exactly what succession means.

What Does Succession Planning Look Like?

While the drama and fanfare that HBO has brought to succession may be entertaining, it is not what we see as an effective example of planning for law firms. Succession is the process of the timely and effective transfer of clients and leadership to the firm's next generation. Succession planning is establishing a program that does this successfully. An effective succession program acts as a set of guidelines implemented by the firm to ensure continuation of service from retiring attorneys to the next team or lawyer who will continue to serve the firm and its clients. Succession planning focuses on the future of the firm while building on its past success. A clear and comprehensive succession program is vital to the continuation of the firm and its future success. Its foundation is the firm's culture. Understanding the culture is important as it serves as the basis to a succession plan that can live successfully within the firm's evolving environment. Additionally, succession plans can be formal or informal, flexible, but always captured in writing to avoid misunderstandings and reduce erroneous interpretations.

Comprehensive succession programs begin with the firms hiring process, so planning begins here as well. While it seems young lawyers no longer stay with firms as long as they have in the past, it is still important to hire with the mindset that these lawyers will commit to a successful firm and grow into a leadership role, someday running the firm. Regardless of their tenure, new lawyers are responsible for and contribute to overall client retention and firm health. Recruitment and searches should always include attention to the skills, qualifications, and leadership abilities that the firm believes will assist the firm in maintaining its plan, persisting, and flourishing. Interviews and hiring conversations should include elements of how potential attorneys fit into or add value to the firm's long-term plan. Firm mindset continues to be important during the post-hiring period as well. Mentoring lawyers and training them on the importance of succession begins once they join the firm. That means firm cultures that continue to recognize and reward teamwork, collaboration, and loyalty from all lawyers create environments that support succession.

An effective succession program establishes how the plan meets the needs of the clients, the lawyers, and the firm. All these groups need to be informed as to why succession is important, what role they play in it, and how they can assist in its success. Clear communication and collaboration are essential. Succession planning is a process. We know it is not quick and easy. We also know it is vital to the long-term success of the firm.

Primary Benefits of Succession Planning

We know that law firms who invest the time and energy into drafting a strong succession program are far more effective in transitioning the management of the firm than those who leave it to circumstance and strong personalities. We also know that the unity and sustainability an adopted succession plan provides helps firms keep good clients—the kind of clients they want. When your firm's EV is running quietly, is looking good, and is well-maintained, a client is more likely to hitch a ride in the passenger seat. Three factors to consider in succession planning are clients, lawyers, and the firm. Specific benefits of this process are also apparent to the retiring lawyers if done effectively and timely.

Clients

Attracting High Quality Clients

Sustained quality service is a trademark of a stable and successful firm. When there is an established succession program in place to ensure clients are served beyond the initial relationship of the lead attorney, clients can have confidence that their relationship with the firm is valuable. The firm's investment in succession planning strengthens trust in current and potential clients and any investment made by the client bolsters the firm. This mutual benefit acts as an inherent enhancement in marketing—propelling firm reputation and enhancing the firm's ability to attract and retain quality clients.

Retaining High Quality Clients

The firm and its retiring lawyers can more easily retain quality clients when seasoned lawyers have a positive working relationship with growing lawyers in the firm. Display of these relationships allows clients to see that the firm has a long-term service strategy in place which reduces questions and concerns from clients about their own investment in the client-firm relationship. While we know that internal relationship building for succession is an important aspect of a program, it is also a key benefit as it helps retain quality clients.

Lawyers

Attracting and Retaining High Quality Lawyers

High quality lawyers join successful firms. Successful firms are built by high quality lawyers. For a firm to attract good lawyers, firms need to have good lawyers. This cycle is addressed during succession planning. To retain good lawyers, firms not only need to have a plan to keep them but a program that functions to carry out that plan. Strong succession programs intentionally include actionable items that—upon completion—result in quality lawyers choosing to stay with the firm, help scaffold its success, and enthusiastically recruit and mentor new lawyers capable of continuing the cycle.

Developing Consistent Leadership and Legal Services

Good lawyers become successful lawyers that build successful firms, in part, through the mentoring and training they receive from within the firm. Effective succession programs that include plans for facilitating mentorship and providing purposeful training helps good lawyers develop into successful lawyers with the skills, knowledge, and experience necessary to provide exemplary service and serve as firm leaders.

Transitioning and Retiring Leaders

While succession may not be simple for the firm, it is perhaps even more difficult for the retiring lawyer who may have spent their entire professional career serving his/her clients and investing in the firm. In succession, those who initially founded or maintained this successful firm are now asked to transition their clients and their roles in the firm on to the next generation. Doing so effectively requires mutual trust and respect. Collaborating with firm leaders to determine how to meet their needs during this time is key in succession planning. For example, actively engaging retiring leaders could come in the form of mentoring or training less-experienced lawyers—giving them an important role outside of practicing law. Or ceremonial acknowledgment of a valuable career that made a difference to the firm could also be a way to give back to those who came before.

Firm

Strengthening Through Preparedness

Firms that adopt a program that is flexible and addresses special circumstances are prepared to withstand emergencies. For instance, a responsible attorney may suddenly be unavailable to represent their clients due to circumstances that they may not have foreseen; however, with a succession program in place that addresses myriad special circumstances, a plan can quickly be enacted to prevent disruption in client service. Succession programs not only provide a sense of preparedness in terms of the long-term organization of the firm but can also be effective in both singular instances of potential disruption—like lawyer health—or in multipronged crisis like pandemics, natural disasters, and political unrest.

Formulating Long-Term Firm Success

Comprehensive firm strategic planning provides goals, objectives, and strategies for success; specifically, it helps firms identify short-term and long-term goals. For firms with goals of long-term success, implementation of their succession program should be part of strategic planning. Implementation will create a structured, future-focused, and nimble environment where success can develop, continue to grow, and be consistent over time.

Safeguarding Long-Term Firm Financial Health

Firms equipped with succession plans—and therefore the preparedness necessary—are positioned for good long-term financial health and well-being. Succession programs influence the firm's ability to retain good clients and quality lawyers. It also influences the firm's ability to hire and retain mindful and meticulous money managers which in turn helps firms stay financially healthy long-term.

Drawing Out Overlooked or Unconscious Biases

As mentioned above, law firm succession planning is challenging. Program development and implementation can also *be challenged* by internal and external circumstances, values, and priorities—in many cases these are overlooked at first or not recognized. We know that not having succession plans can cause a firm to be at risk for business disruption, client attrition, attorney departures or attrition, the inability to effectively serve clients, a reduction of firm profit, the loss of revenue, the lack of qualified lawyer recruitment, a lack of firm vision, a lack of firm leadership, the lack of pro-active planning, and potential malpractice claims. Recognizing and acknowledging potential obstacles to planning allows the firm to be prepared to address its weaknesses and threats. A comprehensive succession program can provide strength and opportunities to address both foreseen and unforeseen issues in planning efforts. Some challenges include:

- **A lack of interest in the firm's future.** If the firm's culture does not encourage team, cooperative client service, and firm first vision, it is likely that some lawyers' own needs will take priority over the needs of the firm leading to a low degree of interest in the firm's future.
- **No clear understanding of the roles in management.** Who oversees ensuring the firm's future? If no management role has clear responsibility for succession or the future of the firm, the day-to-day tasks of management can quite often override the vision needed to plan for succession.
- **A lack of mentoring and training of younger lawyers for succession.** Succession programs depend on preparing less-experienced lawyers to succeed to leadership positions within the firm as well as becoming the responsible attorney for client relationships. They must be ready to do both.
- **A lack of desire to involve the next generation in decision making.** Management is sometimes reluctant to be transparent

with the next generation. They don't allow them to learn about the business of the practice of law. The firm is missing an opportunity to shape and mold the next generation to be successful within its management culture. In this instance, management is limited to too few people and loses the ability to grow future leaders.

- **A lack of desire to be involved in management.** Some lawyers simply don't want to be involved in management because it takes too much time away from serving clients.
- **Management roles go unrewarded.** In many firms, management roles are not rewarded and therefore lawyers aren't interested in participating. This can be detrimental to leadership development and the implementation of succession.
- **The firm's complacency regarding the relationship between the responsible attorney and the client.** Often the firm does not monitor client relationships of senior lawyers unless a problem is brought to light. Therefore, the firm is unaware of the relationship status and if the client would be open to the succession of their primary lawyer when the time arrives.
- **Clients unwilling to, or uncomfortable with, working with additional firm lawyers.** Unless the responsible or lead lawyer introduces another lawyer to the client, often-times clients have no experience working with other lawyers in the firm. It is imperative that the responsible/lead lawyer create opportunities for other firm lawyers to develop client relationships.
- **Firm lawyers unwilling to share their client with other firm lawyers, therefore they are not familiar with the retiring lawyer's clients.** If a lawyer is unwilling to work as part of a team or be collaborative with their clients, it can lead to difficulties when it comes time to try to transition that client. Relationships are not built beyond the retiring lawyer.
- **The firm being unaware of the responsible lawyer providing poor legal service.** If the firm is not monitoring or at least aware of client relationships, it is difficult to know if the legal services provided have met the client's standards. Often, if a lawyer indicates they are retiring and a client has not been satisfied with the work, they will look to another firm rather than transition to a new lawyer within the same firm.
- **Partner compensation program leads to hording work.** Depending on the firm's compensation program, lawyers may horde work

rather than delegate work to the best advantage of the firm. If this is the case, succession is difficult.

- **An unfair or ineffective succession/transition compensation program.** If the firm does not create a fair compensation program as part of the overall firm succession program it will not encourage retiring lawyers to transition their clients and retire. It will incentivize them to stay at the firm, keep their clients and then leave when it best fits them.
- **Lack of successor lawyer for the client.** Sometimes it is difficult for a retiring lawyer to identify a successor lawyer for their clients. It can be emotional, especially if they wait until they are almost ready to retire. Again, if the firm is not monitoring relationships, they are unprepared for this issue.
- **The responsible lawyer being unaware of their own clients' needs and leadership transition.** Serving clients shouldn't be done with blinders on. However, some lawyers don't see past the issues directly in front of them. Succession doesn't only take place in law firms, but in client businesses as well. For law firm succession to work, client business succession must be understood and planned for as well.

Concrete Approaches and Strategies to Jumpstart

When developing an effective succession program there are several facets of succession for small to mid-sized law firms to consider prior to beginning the work. It is imperative that these discussions are had in an organized and focused manner to avoid creating a narrowly focused process that only addresses part of the issue or deals with the immediate and not the future. Remember, an effective plan is flexible, addresses special circumstances, values culture, and ebbs and flows with different economic environments. It involves understanding current culture, imagining what we want future firm culture to look like, drafting a blueprint, and agreeing on a process for how to construct it.

Draft the Goals of the Succession Program

Assemble a dedicated, representative group that asks: What is the firm hoping to achieve? What role does the program play in the overall strategic plan of the firm? Who will be involved with the development and the implementation process? What elements will be included? This group may also tackle thought-provoking questions like those in the introduction:

- Who is driving the private law firm model? Our generation or the next?
- What motivates Millennials and Gen Zs to stay? To work toward ownership?
- Where will the private law firm model be in the next three to five years?
- When will AI change roles in firms? In the profession?
- Why would we change the focus of our marketing efforts?
- How will operations and client service evolve with tech advances?

Establish the Process of Succession Planning

The law firm succession program will not work unless the firm receives buy-in from the lawyers within the firm. The best way to create buy-in is to involve all lawyers in its development. Once the group drafting goals and developing the program has been determined, they should survey the lawyers for input to help identify the important elements of a successful lawyer transition program. Once the draft program has been developed, the feedback loop should be continued again. This shows the group's commitment to buy-in and demonstrates to the other members of the firm that they can be trusted to consider all priorities. Once the final plan has been developed, distribution and implementation should occur in a timely fashion so as not to belabor the effort. The succession of clients and the transition of law firm management will not happen unless everybody agrees that it is important for the continued success of the firm. Both are vital. Everybody is important to the success of the plan.

Communicate Regularly

Make sure everybody is on the same page as the program moves forward. Consider initial input, discuss feedback, share ideas, brainstorm collaboratively, draft, and finalize strategies through open and transparent—but also structured—means. As the program moves into the implementation stages it is also important to involve people who will foster its success.

Remain Future-Focused

Firms may benefit from analyzing current value differences among generations, evolutions in professional culture, advancements in technology, and changes in client expectations when creating and implementing succession. What made the firm successful in the past may not be what will continue to make it successful in the future. Some things, like sound business practices and effective client service strategies, are essential and may transcend shifts in culture; however, cultural trends will always come into play. How interpretation and forecasting of those trends are managed through succession is important—especially when it comes to unlikely or unforeseen issues, or growing differences within the firm. Concepts like work-life balance, flexible work schedules, working from home, ownership expectations, billable hour expectations, and so on, will be topics of conversation that need to be explored and incrementally reviewed overtime—like minding the gauge on your EV's dashboard. Ten years ago, you may not have been able to road trip in a battery-powered vehicle, but now the charging station infrastructure has been built to make that possible. You wouldn't want to forgo a travel opportunity in 2025 because you were under the impression that charging station infrastructure still looked like it did in 2015.

Be Financially Responsible

The financial planning aspect of the succession program is essential to its success. The program must reward the retiring lawyer as well as the successor lawyer, but not put the firm in a precarious financial position. The financial element of the client transition program can be flexible depending on the specific situation of the retiring lawyer; however, guidelines can be instituted as part of the overall program and stewarded accordingly. Generally, as a lawyer begins to transition their clients, they are rewarded for implementing that transition of clients and the successor lawyer is rewarded for doing the work for that client. Both need to be recognized in a system that is fair and equitable. The retiring lawyer is only rewarded if clients are transitioned. Ceding client control is difficult but must happen if a transition is to take place. The goal is to keep the client in the firm.

Some leaders who are retiring from the firm may be reluctant to give up their decision-making roles in management; however, this must happen for leaders to grow and gain experience in the business of the practice of law. Many firms do provide a small stipend to lawyers who are willing to become successor leaders when they take on leadership roles. As senior leaders reduce their time and successor leaders take on more responsibility, compensation for these roles can transition as well.

Ideas to Integrate

Elements of a Management Transition Plan

As mentioned earlier in this chapter, culture plays a major role in the development and implementation of the firm management succession/transition program. Succession strategies must be developed with firm culture in mind. A first-generation law firm that has not previously transitioned management can sometimes be more hesitant to *give up* decision-making authority and visioning. They believe they are the most qualified to maintain control of the vision, planning, and financial strategies and have not included the next generation in these functions. This lack of collaboration and exclusive practice can inhibit the effective transfer of leadership when it becomes necessary. It is important for current senior management to recognize the need for more inclusion and take steps to ensure the transition for future success. Involving the next generation of leaders in management early is an essential element of successful transitioning. Remember, as stated before, effective hiring is the first step in a successful succession/transition plan.

Identifying Future Leaders

When it comes to law firm management, identifying future leaders is perhaps the most important element of succession planning. Asking, listening to, and observing young lawyers and pinpointing those who demonstrate the interest, drive, skills, and abilities needed to become effective firm managers is essential for both their success and the future firm's success. Leaders must not only possess commitment, determination, and positive performance but must also have the personality, respect, and trust that will allow them to be effective in the role.

Before identifying these attributes in young lawyers, the firm must first agree upon them. Again, a group should be identified to take on this task. A description of each management position should be drafted and include input from the rest of the firm. The description(s)—which would include the skills, abilities, and responsibilities of each position—may, in part, be based on the evaluation of current senior leaders who have been a successful component of the firm.

As the process of choosing future leaders begins, consider all young lawyers as candidates for management positions. As the process moves forward and they are compared to the positions and the traits needed, eliminate those lawyers who do not meet the criteria established. During their tenure with the firm, the young lawyers' committee work, marketing ability, legal skills, collaboration, adherence to firm expectations, individual core values vs firm core values, and other specifics should be considered.

Firm managers are leaders of the firm. They must possess the ability to gain support for their ideas (as well as others'), build internal relationships, and gain the trust of those they lead. Personality plays a large role in their ability to do this. Questions that could be considered when determining this might include:

- Does this person have the respect of leaders in the firm?
- Does this person treat other people with respect, regardless of their position in the firm?
- Do they share the core values of the firm? How have they displayed them?
- Do their actions match their words?

Firm mentoring programs provide an optimal avenue by which to identify future leaders. In effective mentor programs the mentor should be able to help the firm evaluate the leadership skills of their mentee. They can provide input regarding whether the mentee meets the expectations and qualifications the firm is looking for in their leaders—and importantly, concrete examples of how.

Preparing Future Leaders

Once identified, future leaders may be invited to get involved in management. This involvement should be strategic and intentional. An organized and structured introduction to management provides a win-win situation where less-experienced lawyers may slowly gain more experience while firm leaders remain in control of what information is accessed. This also allows current leaders to prepare young lawyers in accordance with the firm management culture. Involving strong management candidates in some form of firm management after 3–4 years with the firm may seem early, but it is imperative for the stability of the firm's succession program. Steps to consider:

1. When a young lawyer joins the firm, require them to develop a personal practice plan. Ensure they know that they have support from their mentor or other firm leaders in the drafting process. The initial plan should include details on how they will develop their legal

practice over the next two years. As they make progress on their plan, be sure to assess it with them. Remind mentees to update it regularly including narrative of their growth and accomplishments. Narrative and the supporting details help the firm to understand their ability for vision, implementation, pro-active steps, reflection, etc.

2. After the first two years with the firm, a secondary plan or revised plan may be developed. To increase their participation and platform for displaying their abilities, assign them to committees where they can provide input regarding the business of the practice of law. Observe their behavior, their participation, how they work with others, and their thoughts on issues such as technological advances, substantive practice groups, marketing, etc.
3. Then, involve them in the recruitment of new associates. The hiring process is a very important aspect of the firm's business operations. This engagement allows them to see the process holistically. They will learn what the firm looks for in its lawyers and why those characteristics are considered. They will also gain experience thinking through the firm's core values and how to put them into practice. Additionally, they can begin envisioning how they would run this process in the future.
4. Involve them in the orientation, mentoring, and training program for associates. Having been through the process, they can provide input and ideas to improve the current process or help develop one where a current program does not yet exist.
5. When it becomes appropriate, begin to share the business of the practice of law including some aspects of the financial strategies of firm management. Teach them the *why*. While they have been receiving their own billing hours, for example, now they can begin to receive firm financial information to gain a better understanding of overall business operations.
6. Begin to involve them in marketing and public relations. While developing client relationships through their legal practice, allow them to grow additional relationships as an upcoming leader within the firm. They can tag along with the managing partner (MP) or management committee members when they are conducting firm business. This allows them to observe and learn what it takes to deal with outside vendors, how to negotiate contracts, and other business-related tasks.

7. Include associates and young lawyers in all—or part of—the firm's strategic planning efforts and the annual firm retreat. This allows them to observe how partners interact with each other, how decision-making works, and to understand what really happens in the business of the practice of law.

Management Transition Summary

Management can often make or break a law firm. Strong, effective, and focused management is not an accident, and it doesn't automatically transition to the next generation. Create a program that ensures the firm continues successfully. Remember:

- Firm succession begins when you hire young lawyers: hire lawyers who fit the firm culture and who meet the firm leadership criteria.
- Succession doesn't begin at the end, but starts at the beginning of a lawyer's career.
- Be focused, consistent, and organized.
- Create programs that will help young lawyers build their management and leadership skills.
- Identify who will lead the young lawyer development program.
- Firm training programs ensure that training is mutually beneficial for both the trainee and the firm.
- Assess regularly.
- Give authority along with responsibility.

Don't Forget

While the firm management succession plan focuses on the future, the firm must not discount the past. Many senior lawyers have given so much of their time, energy, and knowledge to build the firm. This needs to be recognized. A strong succession plan must assist the lawyers' transition away from leadership and management positions for without them success might have been lost.

A professional practice plan must also be developed and implemented for the transition of the management leader whether it be back to full-time legal practice, out of the practice of law, or to some other role within the firm. The transition plan may include:

- Creating a gradually increasing billable hour plan that includes returning to the legal practice and building a client base. A timeframe would be established, and a compensation program agreed upon. The process would be evaluated regularly and modified if necessary.

- If the transitioning lawyer does not want to practice law, identify other roles within the firm where they can provide value. Many transitioning lawyers act as mentors to the young lawyers and help the firm develop future leaders. There is an agreed upon hour expectation and compensation for this arrangement.
- Identify any unique ability—legal or otherwise—the firm can leverage to enhance either management or client service, this could include being a PR person or a marketing expert to help with visibility and the reputation of the firm.
- Perhaps there are special projects the firm needs to address, but don't have the manpower for current management or lawyers to perform. The transitioning lawyer could lead short-term projects for the firm.

Elements of a Client Transition Plan

A firm is not a business without clients. Clients will come and clients will go. But some will remain long term if you have the right succession/transition program in place. Compensation may seem like an elephant in the room. It is common for firms to consciously or unconsciously avoid conversations on compensation to keep a sort of peace; however, if the firm's compensation system does not reward collaborative, team-building, firm-focused behavior, succession is going to be much more difficult. Make an educated effort to address compensation before the quiet silences the success of your firm. Another common point of avoidance: selfishness. If the firm culture has developed lawyers with a sole focus on their own success, greed, and personal gain, succession is going to be a problem. Likewise, if the firm does not mentor their young lawyers to understand the importance of acknowledging senior leaders' significance, secession is going to be a problem. Mutuality is key.

Developing and implementing an effective client succession/transition program is both an individual lawyer responsibility and a firm responsibility. Both the firm having an organized and focused program and the individual transitioning lawyer understanding and being willing to transition clients for a win-win-win (client, lawyer, firm) situation are vital for success. A commitment to client retention is important. An understanding of the roles that must be played and a timeline and process must be agreed upon for everything to work smoothly. That includes the client as well. Client succession programs do not happen overnight. Most programs take at least five years to fully implement. Which means lawyers who are thinking about retiring within that time frame should notify the firm and the process should begin—at least a discussion should begin. Some firms identify an age at which the discussion begins, regardless of whether a lawyer has indicated retirement thoughts. Whatever a program includes, the process must begin at some point and the program must identify how.

Long-Term Client Transition Includes

Strong orientation, mentoring, and training programs. The implementation of these is essential and have proven to better prepare young lawyers to serve clients faster, more effectively, and more skillfully than those firms who let young lawyers "learn in the trenches."

Collaborative service teams. Once a client has been brought on board, they should be assigned a secondary lawyer (preferably a young lawyer). This allows for better communication should the primary lawyer be unavailable. Assigning a team also helps develop a more comprehensive relationship with that client. The responsible/primary lawyer would lead the team, driving the service strategy, etc. This allows young lawyers to learn and the firm to be in a position of preparedness for unexpected situations and long-term transition.

Client education. It is also important that the client understand the firm's service mentality and why it benefits them. Prepare a description of the team serving the client and provide it to the client. When initially meeting with the client, the team should be present. After the initial meeting, strategically plan who the client should interact with most to their benefit. Keep all team members in front of the client at some point. Include younger lawyers in various situations both in legal service tasks as well as social settings, helping to develop an overall relationship with clients. This also teaches them how to interact with clients at all levels.

Create a bank of training hours for young lawyers. The hours can be used for training situations like those above when they can't really bill for their time, but is a learning opportunity. Ensure that at least one young lawyer is assigned to become experienced in each significant practice within the firm, especially if that practice is predicted to continue to be a profitable practice within the firm. Build the skills for those practices within the younger generation. It will take time, plan for it.

Pay attention to the years of practice of the lawyers in the firm. Review on an annual basis to ensure there is not a gap between years of experience leading to an inability for the firm to transition a practice to the next generation of lawyers. Sometimes, firms realize too late that there is significant difference in skill and expertise from the older generation to the next. As an example, a senior lawyer wants to retire, has a great practice, but realizes there is no lawyer in the firm who has enough knowledge, skill, and experience to receive the practice and there is not enough time to train a young lawyer for the role.

Be aware of your clients' business and leadership plans. Often, firms are unaware that long-term clients are implementing their own leadership succession plans. When that happens, they review their legal representation, and the new leadership may consider new legal relationships. Be on top of this through the firm's succession program when reviewing top clients. Ensure the successor lawyer to the client has a relationship with the next generation in the client business.

Focused Transition Includes

- Every two years, assign somebody in the firm to review the firm's top clients. Identify who the primary attorney is for each client. This provides the firm with an understanding of who their top clients are and who is responsible for them. If those clients are being served by an attorney who will be transitioning out in the next five years, a discussion should take place.
- Once a lawyer has identified their retirement plans, create a plan to be followed including a timetable and the steps to be taken. The plan might include:
  - ❒ Constructing a matrix of the top clients and their expectations and needs;
  - ❒ Creating a list of referral sources with a plan to introduce them to the successor lawyer;
  - ❒ Providing help to train the successor if specialized training is necessary;

    - ❒ Involving the successor with social events with the clients, including them with court proceedings, depos, signings; using training hours to assist in transition, etc.;
    - ❒ Scheduling meetings with the successor lawyer to enhance communication during the transition process;
    - ❒ Communicating with the clients regarding the successor lawyer and encouraging the relationship.
- The firm and the transitioning attorney must identify the lawyer(s) who will be the successor lawyer(s) to each client. Sometimes the retiring lawyer will have clients who bridge different practices and will be served in the future by different lawyers.
- Develop a compensation program that rewards the retiring lawyer. The program must be fair and recognize their efforts while also being fair to the firm without putting it in financial worry.
- Consider what, in addition to compensation, the retiring lawyer might receive from the firm, if anything.
- As indicated previously, create the plan for the retiring lawyer. Put it in writing so everybody understands the roles to be played.
- Assess and evaluate the plan consistently and update as necessary.

When developing a firm succession program, the focused elements of the plan should act as the guidelines for all retiring lawyers. In other words, the firm succession plan should indicate what the compensation program would be for each retiring lawyer. However, given individual situations, it should be flexible to recognize special circumstances. The special circumstances, however, should not become the norm.

Client Transition Summary

Remember:

- Focus, plan, and organize—and do it early;
- Mentor and train successor lawyers for success;
- Help successor lawyers build client relationships;
- Identify young lawyers who can be successful with specific clients;
- Begin the transition when the client joins the firm—be collaborative, team-oriented, and client-focused for firm success;
- Help the primary/retiring lawyer to be comfortable, recognize their contribution, and reward them appropriately;
- Make it a win-win-win.

Conclusions

Law firm leaders have so many things to think about when it comes to championing successful business operation strategies. The development and implementation of a law firm succession program is challenging. Implementing the plans—even more tricky. While a firm can craft a generic program, implementing a plan may vary from lawyer to lawyer as they retire from the firm. So, it is imperative that your firm's program be both flexible and comprehensive—drafting a program that acknowledges succession is not a one-size-fits-all plan. It is, however, one size that fits the firm.

In this chapter, I provide some thoughts and ideas to help you develop a comprehensive succession program that can be a guide as to what needs to be done to prepare clients, lawyers, and the firm for succession. Reestablishing succession planning not as a singular effort, but as a component of an overall long-term strategic success strategy will help encourage the creation of a culture where the lawyers/owners want the firm to succeed beyond their own careers.

Invest in the young, they are our future. Recognize the people who have spent a lifetime dedicated to the practice of law, we wouldn't be here without them. Meld them together to serve clients who need us.

Quit driving your EV around in circles. Plug in: Ask, what does succession planning look like in your firm? Charge up: Answer the question with collaborative input. Put it in drive: Carry out your plans. Arrive at: firm success.

Chapter 14
Generation to Generation

Daniel J. Caruso

I have a confession to make. I really enjoy practicing law. The intellectual and emotional satisfaction one garners from taking on and solving a client's problem, representing them in court, or merely giving trusted advice is just good for the soul. Notice I said "enjoy" not "enjoyed" because even after 50 years, the enjoyment is still there and is burnished by a good deal of knowledge gained over that half-century.

Retirement, or as one of partners used to say, "the R word," is not easy for a lawyer. As we progress through the years, we often are forced to give up things we do: maybe an aching back limits your golf game, your plans to travel have been scuttled by other financial needs, and maybe you shouldn't really be driving at night. Giving up what you do is easy. Giving up what you are is so much harder. And . . . often unnecessary.

The Retirement Plan

Virtually every law firm of any size has a retirement plan, which is another way of saying every firm has a plan to move the old folks out so the younger folks can take over. There is absolutely nothing wrong with that unless the plan inures to the detriment of the firm as opposed to benefiting it. A plan that sends a 65-year-old attorney with substantial billings and client contacts out the door is just plain, okay I will say it, STUPID. Any plan of movement has to make sense in the context of the firm in which it operates. And, while it might have short-term appeal to the younger generation, it's just like that tattoo you got on your back when you were 20, it is going to get old along with you and may not look so good as the years go on. The short-term demands of the few cannot outweigh the long-term benefits to the firm as a whole.

However, time and tide waits for no man and there might come a day when withdrawal from the partnership is required. At that point, those individuals who now comprise the makeup of the firm might want to consider an alternative employment relationship with the firm partnership. One that benefits all.

This is not to say that all aging (for the purpose of this chapter, we will be using 65 or older as defined by the Council for Aging) are valuable assets to which the firm should cling. Partnership mistakes are sometimes made and forced retirement is the surest way to cure those mistakes.

Why Can't We All Get Along

If a retired partner is to remain with the firm, under what conditions would such a relationship remain beneficial? Here are some suggestions for you "golden agers" trying to remain active in the practice:

- **This is not your firm anymore.** You have withdrawn from the partnership and you have no say on how the business will be run. Maybe you were once the managing partner but you are not the managing partner anymore. If asked, you can offer your advice on firm management; but otherwise don't meddle in things that no longer concern you. Soon you will realize how pleasant this is and the temptation to interfere with the management side of the firm controlled by the younger generation will ebb and then cease.
- **Client relations.** By now, you should have already done everything you can to connect your existing clients with your successors. If not, get on with it, you are not going to live forever. And, in spite of the admonition contained in subpart (a), you should be willing to assist any attorney in the development of new business, if asked. You can't teach an old dog new tricks, but there are tricks to be learned from an old dog.
- **Mentoring.** This should go without saying. While this is the world of the iPhone, laptop, Instagram accounts and whatever, experience gained in decades of practice has not been devalued to zero. To discard the hard-earned knowledge gained by an experienced attorney over years would be like destroying a first edition of War and Peace and replacing it with the Kindle version. Subject to the desires of the firm, mentoring could take the form of one-on-one conferences with attorneys who simply have a problem to full-blown seminars where

everyone details their experiences, problems, and frustrations and learns that there is really very little new under the sun.

Compensation

You have finally arrived at a point in your life where monetary pressures have eased. Hopefully, you have a nice fat 401K, the kids are all through college, the beach house is paid for, or at least manageable, and you can put aside the stresses that are now affecting the younger people in your office. No one is saying you should work for free and a reasonable compensation scheme can always be worked out. In considering what the compensation would look like, the firm should value your contribution and you should value the fact that you are allowed to continue doing what you love to do in the presence of those you want to be with. Spoiler alert: the very fact that you don't have a billing target is worth a lot.

The Work

At this point in your career, it should only be about the work. You are not climbing the partnership ladder anymore or fighting your partners for more money or a larger office. That's all over. Take a deep breath. Now, you can truly focus on the pure quality of the work you are doing or assisting others in improving their work. You now have the time to study that Supreme Court case or to even explore areas of the law in which you might be interested, but never actually practiced. You are still associated with the firm and perhaps can even attend court for a particular client when your presence might be of assistance to a younger attorney. How about reviewing and editing memoranda and briefs? Attending depositions? Document review? Or, helping out that firm member who wants to see his daughter's softball game.

A whole world of opportunities has been opened to you from which you and your younger colleagues can benefit. You simply have to look for them.

And Now Some Words for the Next Generation

The law firm where you now work was built on the blood, sweat, (and in some cases) tears of people, some of whom you never met, some of whom you never even heard of. Your job is different. You have been given a gift, an opportunity. It is up to you to maintain the reputation of the firm built by your predecessors, and to grow the firm for your own professional and economic benefit. As you already know, it isn't always that easy.

Thinking you are smarter than that old person down the hall is not new. If fact, it's as old as time itself. That problem you have been struggling with for the last two days may not be as hard as you think. Hours of legal research may be expended on looking for the answer. The real irony, of course, is that the answer may be right down the hall in the one information source not connected to any computer. The answer may not be what you want to hear; it may not even be right, but it may at least set you on the right path.

We realize, of course, that many changes have taken place in the practice of law over the last ten to 20 years. Unless you are on the television show "Suits," the men in the office are no longer wearing them. That beautiful library which was the showplace of your office, is now gone in favor of Westlaw and Lexus Nexis. Instagram, X (formerly Twitter) and Facebook are all fertile ground for investigative materials, since people have been engaged in a never-ending quest to shed every bit of privacy they once had. No more getting on an airplane when you can Zoom that deposition, and files your legal assistant once stacked on your desk are now stored in a computer and backed up in someplace known as "the cloud." We get that. But, given all that, we would suggest that the actual practice of law is no different today than it was 100 years ago. As Lincoln once said: "a lawyer's time and advice is his stock in trade." The ability to think and analyze your way through a legal problem and then provide a solution to that problem is still what it is all about. What greater excitement can there be than the final argument in an important jury trial; what greater anxiety than waiting for the jury to deliver its verdict?

Beyond all that, we, the lawyers, keep order in society. Daniel Webster once said: "justice is the greatest concern of man on earth." Even Shakespeare is often misinterpreted in this quote from Henry VI: "First we kill all the lawyers" was a recognition by The Bard that what any potential tyrant must do to eliminate freedom is to rid society of its lawyers. While we have all of the labor-saving conveniences, are we really that much different than our predecessors whose oath bound them to the constitution and the rule of law as any oath taken by an attorney today? The practice of law is an honorable profession, although not always viewed that way by a cynical public. It is up to all of us to live up to the highest standards of this profession, protect our courts, be civil to one another, be inquisitive, be creative, and give each and every one of our clients our very best. Honest Abe would have wanted it that way.

Chapter 15
Equipping Your Law Firm for the Future

Michael S. Beaver

Many have been the predictors of doom for small to mid-size law firms. Over the last 30 years or so, many observers of the legal business have warned that big law firms would eventually eat up or destroy mid-size firms, and would drive smaller firms into marginal near-irrelevance.

Big law has certainly grown, but doomsayers failed to recognize that the downsides of the big law model (high costs, potential for inefficiency, inflexibility, never-ending adversary conflicts, and the like) have created new opportunities for smaller and mid-size firms. And as these firms have capitalized on the opportunities, they have gained credibility in the marketplace for legal services. Even the largest corporate clients now see smaller firms as important partners in the delivery of legal services. They retain small and mid-size firms for interesting, valuable matters.

The future for small to mid-size law firms is indeed bright. They will continue to compete meaningfully with big firms for some of the best legal work (as well as the best legal talent). Building on this book's individual chapters, following are some of the likely characteristics of the most successful small and mid-size law firms.

Hyper-Focus on Clients

The most successful small to mid-size law firms of the future will be hyper-focused on client relationships. This requires knowing clients well enough to understand their needs and wants, knowing their levels of satisfaction with (and suggestions for improvement on) firm performance, anticipating client needs, and building and nurturing personal relationships.

Successful small and mid-size firms understand and build upon the reasons that clients hire them in the first place. For better or worse, at least two-thirds of the time clients send work to those lawyers with whom they have an existing relationship. There is more to this statistic than meets the eye. Where an "existing relationship" is based on previous matters assigned to the firm, it is obviously critical to understand and build on client satisfaction. As is often said, it is far easier to keep a client than find a new one.

But is there any other way to benefit from the "client relationship" effect? Absolutely yes. Investing in relationships with potential client contacts can pay enormous dividends, although payoffs can be somewhat unpredictable. Clients need to know their potential lawyers before they need them. The more potential clients a lawyer gets to know, the more opportunities will arise. Inevitably some potential client contacts will come calling—some because they have become unsatisfied with (or conflicted out of) existing law firms, and some because they have become truly convinced of another lawyer's (i.e., yours) expertise and attention.

Professional networking is essential to building relationships with potential clients. During the early 2020s pandemic, face-to-face interactions were drastically curtailed, and along with that came the perception by some that the development of in-person relationships is not critical to building and maintaining a client base. The pandemic, however, did not change human nature. It remains true that potential clients are far more likely to give you an opportunity if they *know* you. Successful networking involves a strategic investment. What networking opportunities mesh with your firm's strategy? Are the firm's potential clients situated locally or nationally? Is the firm looking to connect with in-house counsel or small business owners who lack in-house legal resources? Are there non-legal industry groups aligned with the firm's strategic priorities? Are your objectives focused on a particular specialized field? Pick specific networking opportunities accordingly, but never overlook more generalized reputation-building activities (such as LinkedIn or other general marketplaces where your background can be featured and reinforced).

Membership in national and international law networks can create tremendous networking opportunities. Large firms know this. Most have created or joined networks comprised of complimentary firms.

Smaller firms haven't always done the same. Many corporate clients are attracted to a firm that can offer collaboration and referral opportunities, which can offset large international law firms' reach. But perhaps more importantly, the personal involvement of firm lawyers in firm networks provides a difficult-to-equal opportunity for meeting clients and client contacts from around the globe.

Similarly, small and mid-size firms often benefit from referrals by larger firms. There are many matters that large firm lawyers cannot take on, often for conflict reasons but also matters which large firms simply cannot handle economically. It is therefore strategically important for smaller firms and their lawyers to build and nurture relationships with large firm professionals.

Small and mid-size firm lawyers should always be mindful that other lawyers and firms will be attempting to lure their existing clients away using many of these same approaches. This underscores the necessity of maintaining existing client relationships and referral sources.

Know the Reasons Your Clients Hire You and Build on Them

There are well-documented reasons that clients—be they small local businesses or international business behemoths—seek out smaller and mid-size firms. They include:

- Cost savings (lower hourly rates, staffing efficiency, better internal collaboration, lower overhead)
- Faster and more personal service (lawyers who are easier to reach, more direct contact with senior lawyers)
- Specialized expertise or experience (including local practice knowledge)
- Fewer adversary conflicts
- Strategic flexibility in client representation

Not all smaller firms focus on all of these potential advantages. For instance, some small firms have high hourly rates based upon sought-after expertise and results. Others may be focused on highly repetitive work rather than esoteric specialties. Successful small and mid-size firms of the future will know the reasons why clients hire them, and will strategically build on them. Small and mid-size firm advantages can be marketed, but more importantly they must actually be experienced by clients.

Expertly Use the Best Technological Tools

Successful lawyers know that expertise and skill alone do not amount to a competitive advantage. Excellence, expertise, and skill are baseline client expectations, not factors that differentiate your firm from others.

The use of technology in law practice has similarly become a baseline client expectation. At a bare minimum, small and mid-size firms must invest in the technology that drives law practice now and into the future. This includes basic intra-firm technology (reliable, cutting-edge software technology for delivery of client services); use of effective discovery and document management platforms; incorporation of artificial intelligence (AI) tools (more on that below); timekeeping, accounting, and billing software (including the capability to quickly adapt to client e-billing practices); and any other software tools that help maximize client service, efficiency, and security.

The use of AI is already widespread in law practice, yet as of now legal use of AI is not sufficiently advanced to reliably predict its longer-term effects. Some studies have suggested that as many as 20% of small and mid-size firms are using AI on a regular basis. Studies also suggest that clients are more likely to view AI as a useful tool than their law firms do, probably because many businesses have already adopted AI in their operations. While it may be difficult to predict the long-term impact on the practice of law, it can be said with certainty that clients expect their firms to be exploring and using AI in the delivery of services. It will be an exceptional challenge.

Cybersecurity will become even more prominent among a firm's technological tools. Besides the obvious exposures resulting from cybersecurity weaknesses, both clients and insurers are demanding adherence to security standards and are likely to demand much move in the coming years. They aren't wrong—cybersecurity is truly a "bet the enterprise" issue for law firms.

Staff expertise is a challenge for small to mid-size firms. In particular, smaller firms may not be able to employ full-time IT staff. This makes the firm's vendor relationships absolutely vital. Most firms will need to contract for software installation, service, training, and general consulting and advice. The vendors selected by a firm will play an important role in the firm's future.

For many firms—even smaller ones—it will be necessary to employ more technological expertise full time. While many basic intra-firm tech tools have become common, AI and cybersecurity are and will remain cutting-edge issues that firms cannot afford to underplay.

Innovate

Innovation always ranks near the top of client surveys. In particular, in-house law departments want to hire law firms that constantly look for new ways to deliver client value.

Delivering greater efficiency often qualifies as innovation. Yet some of the most important innovative insights occur at a deeper level, focusing on why (as opposed to how) things are done the way they are. As the management guru Peter Drucker supposedly said: "there is nothing so useless as doing efficiently that which should not be done."

Unfortunately it isn't possible to list ways to innovate. After all, if a practice is common enough to be listed, it is probably past the innovation stage. The takeaway for law firms is that innovation in delivering client service and value will ideally become part of the firm's DNA. Innovation must be up to you and your firm.

Small firms are in a great position to be innovators. Larger firms are more likely to become steeped in protocols and methods to the point where neither lawyers nor staff question their continuing usefulness. Those less bound by a "this is the way we do things" mentality are often the most able to try out new ideas and methods. Those who don't spend their time thinking "inside the box" don't have to learn to think out of it.

Innovation is the result of insight, but not usually in a vacuum. Lawyers, and especially law firm leaders, should be well-informed about the ways the business of law is developing. Beyond that, lawyers who desire to innovate will be as informed as possible about general technological development, thinking about ways to use new technologies that perhaps haven't yet occurred to others. And an obvious way to develop a firm's innovative spirit is to reward it. Firm lawyers and staff should be recognized and compensated for innovations large and small.

Attract and Retain the Right Talent

Traditional big firm hiring has been largely credential-based—law school pedigree, prestigious clerkships, impressive references, and the like. Big firms have hired well-credentialed young lawyers in large numbers, then turned them loose under high billable hour requirements and whittled down the pool to the most talented over the course of five or ten years. This approach has a certain inefficiency to it, since many hires were never destined to thrive in a big firm practice. Further, many clients believe that the cost of this approach is mostly borne by them. Hordes of associates are required to work thousands of billable hours, at stratospheric rates, in often inefficient ways.

Smaller and mid-size firms have never had the luxury of this approach. It has always been much more important to focus on talent and firm compatibility as much as credentials or pedigree. The future for these firms lies with building on this approach.

From 2018 to 2023, big law firms hired were outpaced in hiring by smaller and mid-sized firms. Largely as a result of uncertainty about future legal demand, big firms reduced hiring and became more selective. That changed markedly by 2025, as big firms hired more, tightening the legal talent market for all firms.

It can be difficult to compete with the sometimes-astronomical associate salaries paid by the largest firms. Yet small and mid-size firms continue to thrive and attract talent. Obviously money isn't everything.

Smaller and mid-size firms will continue to distinguish themselves in the talent market by using several strategies. Younger lawyers in such firms often have much greater opportunity for client contact and meaningful legal work. The best smaller firms also invest in direct mentoring by more experienced lawyers. Junior lawyers in smaller and mid-size firms often have the potential for greater autonomy in their work. The most successful small and mid-size firm will also make the nurturing of a positive, vibrant culture one of their highest priorities. Applicants pick up on a law firm's culture intuitively, and for many of them it will be a major reason to accept an offer.

Hiring for experience will continue to be an important approach for both junior and more senior lawyers. Small and mid-size firms have always been more open than many large firms to hiring experienced associates, rather than just law school graduates. This will continue to be a focus of successful firms. Even a few years of experience gives a young lawyer not only a better platform for practice, but also a much more refined idea of what they want in a law firm.

As to more senior talent, lateral hiring (meaning partner/owner level acquisitions) will remain a vital tool to growth and success, but should never be an end in itself. The best lateral hires will fit within the firm's existing strategy, and will occur for strategic reasons (such as building on a strategically important or complementary practice area). And cultural considerations should play an even greater role in these hires, as senior lawyers have the potential for a far greater cultural impact—for good or ill—immediately.

Non-lawyer hiring is also critically important to firm success. Non-lawyers greatly affect the firm's client experience. Further, the central role played by technology in the law firm of the future means that a firm must value and invest in technological talent and expertise to the extent they invest in lawyers.

Be Flexible

Clients perceive that smaller to mid-size firms are more flexible and nimble. It is one of the reasons even larger clients will hire smaller firms. Deliver on that expectation. Small and mid-size firms can be less hidebound than their larger counterparts. Small and mid-size firms will need to adapt quickly to changing client expectations, technological developments, developments in the law, the needs and expectations of legal and staff talent, and the rapidly changing law practice environment. As with innovation, flexibility will be in the DNA of the future successful small and mid-size firm.